The Biography of Prophets

Javon Rahman Bertrand

MANIFOLD GRACE
Publishing House LLC

Dedication

I dedicate this book to my prophetic sharpeners, Apostle Alejandro Baldwin and Minister Delta Saulsberry. These two prophetic vessels have challenged, rebuked and strengthened my prophetic gift, call and manifestation.

I dedicate this book to the prophets that I have been allowed to instruct, mentor and father; past, present and future. The students of Watchmen International School of the Prophets and Clarity International Christian University (Awakened Word School of the Prophets) for trusting me as a prophetic echo to help you learn, receive and manifest your prophetic call and destiny.

I dedicate this book to prophets all over the world who have been seeking clarity, a deeper understanding and revelation of what God's prophets and prophetics look like. This book is especially for you.

Table of Contents

Foreword

The Prophet. The gifted, yet cursed, oracle who has been given the burden of speaking the divine secrets of God to man. Many of us have viewed the sacred office through the lenses of tradition, religiosity, and in some cases, ignorance. We oft times have formulated our opinion(s) of these divinely gifted messengers, through our experiences, misconceptions, and misunderstanding of scripture. Yet we live in times, where one of the most misunderstood offices…vocations is needed now. We need the prophets.

In his book, *The Biography of Prophets*, Apostle Bertrand debunks the myths and assumptions we have turned into doctrine regarding the prophet and prophetics. In addition to giving clarity, he lays open the life of the prophet by bringing to life the stories of the prophets of old. Many books speak to what the prophets of old spoke and how God used them to bring healing, deliverance, and hope to His people. Yet in this book, we see the life of the prophet in a way that brings humanity to these men and women, in the midst of them doing superhuman acts. Quite simply, you will begin to see the beautiful struggle that we who are called to the prophetic, must contend with. The struggle of being a conduit and mouthpiece of God…to speak His divine truths, that in some cases His people will reject, and in turn reject you. Through these stories, you will begin to better understand your own story as a prophetic person.

In closing, I would ask that you read this book with prayerful eyes and attentive ears. Understand that as you read the biographies of these mighty servants, God will begin to reveal your story. You will understand the beautiful and intimate exchange that is the prophetic. You will see your story emerge through the lives you read about. My hope is that you will see the common thread throughout each prophet that connects us to them. It is the call that we embrace, the surrender that we accept, and the process that we yield too. I pray that you see the prophet in a greater light; a light that reveals how God speaks through "flawed" vessels words of healing, hope and deliverance. Remember, we need the prophets. We need you.

Blessings,

Alejandro C. Baldwin
Founder, ACTS Ministries

Preface

Really, another book about prophets? Yes. Prophets and the prophetic are subjects that we will never stop learning about. This book, however, is different from other books I have seen. The vision of this book is to give understanding about the life of prophets, things we have been taught about, but do not really know. This book is written to help us gain understanding of the prophet as a person, not just a ministerial persona.

Inside the pages of *The Biography of Prophets* will be what the Holy Scriptures show us about the men and women that carried and released the sound of God in the Earth. No, every prophet mentioned in Scripture is not present in this book, but some of the popular, and not so popular prophets, will be discussed. My hope, as the biographer of the prophets, is to help us understand that the ministry, assignment and life of the prophet is not always what we understand it to be. Also, to help some emerging and even seasoned prophets clarify their assignment as a prophet in the earth.

I feel it absolutely necessary to utilize this introduction to write about things that will be standard through each prophet's biography. There are certain things that ALL prophets have in common. Each prophet has a mandate and mantle while functioning in the anointing of God. Since there is a difference, this introduction will explain those differences.

Mantle, Mandate, Anointing

What is a Mantle? A mantle is your calling/election from God Himself, activated through Jesus Christ and guided by Holy Spirit of God. The Hebrew word meh'el, is one of the words translated mantle, simply meaning robe. In the Bible, men of high rank and the high priest wore mantles/robes. The mantle separates you from everyone else. The kings wore mantles that looked different from the mantle of prophets whose mantles looked different from that of the high priest. Today, we may not wear a mantle in cloth, but all leaders have mantles. Some leaders wear specially designed robes to separate them from other leaders, that is a mantle. Our mantles today are more spiritual than material. Whether it be a prayer shawl or a specially designed robe, it should be respected as holy before God and people. The mantle is significant to the calling and election of the prophet. Before a person takes a mantle and puts it on, they should make their calling and election sure (1 Peter 1:10). Mantles can be passed down from one generation to another. Elijah passed his mantle down to Elisha. After Elisha had proven himself a son and a servant worthy of the mantle, it was released upon him. Mantles are passed down from leadership to sons and daughters.

Mantles are not man-made, they are God-breathed. Every prophet is mantled to carry the sound of Heaven and the voice of God. The mantle comes with a delegated authority and power as given by God. Mantles were known for being made of the highest quality and valued material. This is why they are to be respected as from God and not as God. Every mantle is costly, the blood that was shed, paid for, the person wearing the mantle, and the mantle. We will never be able to put a financial value on the blood, so let us honor what was redeemed, by His blood, for the fulfilling of His kingdom and church.

What is a Mandate?

A mandate is the specified assignment of a person in the earth. The mandate God has assigned to you, operates in conjunction with your mantle and the anointing. Mandates are specific to what God desires you to accomplish in the earth.

Isaiah's mandate was revealed in Isaiah 61:1-2 *...to preach good tidings unto the meek; he hath sent me to bind up the brokenhearted, to proclaim liberty to the captives, and the opening of the prison to them that are bound; To proclaim the acceptable year of the LORD, and the day of vengeance o four God; to comfort all that mourn;*

Jeremiah's mandate was revealed in Jeremiah 1:10 *See, I have this day set thee over the nations and over the kingdoms, to root out, and to pull down, and to destroy, and to throw down, to build, and to plant.*

Isaiah and Jeremiah were both mantled prophets, yet their mandates were different. We may operate in the same office and mantle and our mandates will be different. We have to learn to operate in the networking mind of God. Your mandate may be different from mine, but we can work together to accomplish both mandates. Mandates are tailor-made for individuals. Although, mantles can be passed down, mandates cannot. There may be a group of apostles who have the same mantle, but different anointing and mandates. Every apostle is not a pastor, but all operate in miracles because of the anointing that comes with the mantle of apostleship - for example.

<u>What is the Anointing?</u>

The anointing is what causes the manifestations in your ministry. It is because of the anointing that people are healed, delivered, experience miracles, etc. The anointing is the manifestation of God through us, His people.

The anointing comes along with the mantle you wear. There are certain administrations of the anointing that go along with the mantle. Some anointings, all believers operate under and through (Mark 16:17-18). When a mantle is passed down, so is the anointing that goes with it. When Elijah passed down his mantle to Elisha, Elisha began to operate in certain things that Elijah had operated in. I personally have passed a prayer mantle to an individual, and the manifestations and the anointing that flowed through me in prayer, now operates in them.

The difference between a mantle, an anointing and a mandate is clear: the mantle is the graced calling and election that came before the foundation of the world. The anointing is the operation and manifestation of the Holy Spirit through the people of God. The mandate is the specific assignment that will be completed under the mantle of the person. Now, I must ask, do you know your mantle, anointing and mandate in the earth? If not, you need to be led of God to a ministry that can reveal it and train you in those areas.

There is only ONE anointing and it is administered differently through each gift. Holy Spirit carries the only anointing in the land and we as sons of God manifest in different administrations (1 Corinthians 12, Romans 12, Ephesians 6) for the profit of all.

Prophets are one administration of Holy Spirit and the

anointing of God. They carry an authority, a weight, and the sound of Heaven like none other. As ambassadors of God's communication to His creation, prophets echo God's word, law, vision, and kingdom in the earth. Prophets may be the oldest ministerial function (gift) upon the earth but it has also been the most misunderstood, mistreated and dishonored. God is bringing clarity to His prophetic order, that the Body of Christ can be returned to wholeness in Him. As you read these biographies, open your mind to the reality of God's prophets and prophetics in the 21st century.

Why are Prophets Important?

"In the beginning God ([a] Elohim) [b] created [by forming from nothing] the heavens and the earth. ²The earth was [c] formless and void or a waste and emptiness, and darkness was upon the face of the deep [primeval ocean that covered the unformed earth]. The Spirit of God was moving (hovering, brooding) over the face of the waters. ³And God said, [d] "Let there be light"; and there was light." (Genesis 1:1-3 AMP)

We are beginning in Genesis to establish that God speaks and is still speaking to His earth and His people. There is no prophecy without God; for prophecy belongs to Him and is established in His dwelling, Heaven.

Before we can deal with Prophets, we must consider who called them, sent them and why they were sent. God, Elohim, has a great desire to communicate with His creation. He is the God of Communication (Hallelujah!). As Almighty God wants to speak to His creation, He has created multiple forms of communication; *from Him to us* and *from us to Him.* Prophets are His communication ambassadors. They are called and sent to carry His mind, strategy and purpose to those who dwell in the earth.

Prophecy is God speaking from a settled word in Heaven, to an earth still working towards destiny. Prophecy is God expressing His supreme knowledge into the earth.

Almighty God uses His words to create! He uses His words to deliver and transform! He uses His words to answer, correct, align and position! God does not use words that cannot manifest as He spoke them. Every word God speaks has purpose according to Isaiah 55:11 which states:

*So shall my word be that goeth forth out of my mouth: it shall not return unto me void, but it shall **accomplish** that which I please, and it shall **prosper** in the thing whereto I sent it.*

His word must accomplish and it must prosper. God is in the business of doing and being fruitful (*the actual meaning of prosper*).

The basis of all communication is words. Prophets communicate God's words to His people, not their own. Communication is defined as the act or process of using words, sounds, signs, or behaviors to express or exchange information or to express your ideas, thoughts, feelings, etc., to someone else. Communication is a discourse. Discourse is the use of words to exchange thoughts and ideas. Communication (prophecy) will cause a discourse between God and His people, Heaven and Earth.

God's Communication Styles (A Short List)
1. *Audible Voice – Genesis 1-3; Isaiah 28:23*
2. *Still Small Voice (Whisper) – First Kings 19:11-12*
3. *Singing – Zephaniah 3:17*
4. *Visual Communication*
   a. *Visions – Matthew 17:9, Acts 9:10-12*
   b. *Dreams – Genesis 28:12; Matthew 1:25; Jude 1:8-9*

c. Trances – Acts 10:8-11; Acts 11:5

5. *Laughing – Psalm 37:13*
6. *Through Angels – Genesis 32:24-31; Acts 10:1-6*
7. *Writing – Exodus 31:18*

<u>Our Communication Styles To God (A Short List)</u>
1. *Obedience (Deuteronomy 28:1-14; 1 Samuel 15:22; Hebrew 5:8)*
2. *Prayer (2 Kings 19:4; 2 Chronicles 6:19-20; James 5:15-16)*
3. *Worship (Genesis 22:5; Psalm 95:6; John 4:20-24; Colossians 3:16)*
4. *Fasting (2 Chronicles 20:1-18; Acts 10)*
5. *Singing (Psalm 96:1; Psalm 98:1; Psalm 149:1)*
6. *Meditation of Our Heart (Psalm 19:14)*
7. *Unknown Tongues (1 Corinthians 14:2)*

God uses these communication styles to speak to His believers and His prophets. As we gain an understanding of His ways of communication, we also see how prophets are used to deliver His word.

When prophets speak they release the voice and mind of God into the earth. Prophets are the spokesmen of God and Heaven. They carry the language and sound of God into the earth. Not speaking of themselves prevents prophets from becoming gods to the people. Prophets echo God in all that they do. As well as being spokesmen, prophets are ambassadors of the Kingdom of God. As an ambassador, prophets carry the health of the kingdom. Carrying health, the ministry of prophets brings healing, cures and soundness of mind to those that receive God's word. The word of God is to bring man to wholeness, whether through repentance or obedience to the word.

Prophets are raised, not by what they have accomplished

in the earth, but by the purposes of God before the beginning of time. There is nothing a person can do to become a prophet. Prophets come into the earth and have to learn and accept their eternal call for an earthly destiny. Every prophet comes into the reality of his or her prophethood differently, but God always affirms it. Some prophets are graced with more than one mantle for the glory of God and the establishment of His government. Prophets can also be writers, teachers, function in government and business, be married and a multiplicity of other things. Prophets cannot be boxed in, nor should they be restricted by the thoughts of man or false traditions of what prophets do. Prophets do not speak from their nature knowledge, they speak from the Supreme Knowledge of God. No prophecy is at the will of man, it is breathed and inspired by God Himself.

Prophets are like snowflakes, each unique in their function and purpose in the earth. No two prophets are exactly like and God did that purposely. Throughout scripture we see prophets in many forms and doing various things at the instruction of the Lord. Every prophet will not have a major platform to nations, but every prophet has a mandated assignment in the earth. Some prophets prophesy very often, while others every so often; still both are prophets. Some prophets travel extensively while others are used only in one locale, both are still prophets. Some teach in church settings, while others in government and another sect will prophesy in business arenas, all still prophets. We have to learn that prophets are more than church preachers. God is not restricted to the church and neither are His prophets.

Prophets, do not get caught in the hype of going to the nations. Every prophet is not assigned, graced or purposed to go to the nations. Some prophets are local, regional, national, international and few are global. Learn your assignment, embrace it and walk it out. Do not let subterfuge convince you that you are not good enough because of what others may be doing by God's will, or not.

Debunk: expose the falseness or hollowness of (a myth, idea, or belief): the magazine that debunks claims of the paranormal. (New Oxford American Dictionary)

Chapter One:

The Chapter of Debunking

Many of us have erred, flawed and disappointing understandings of prophets and the prophetic. For years, we have repetitively heard misinterpreted teachings, clichés and false messages about them. As Holy Spirit is preparing us for an amazing move with Him, we need to understand His prophets. We have to have proper knowledge to know how to labor with and receive His prophets and the benefit of this ministry gift. It is my goal to utilize this chapter to debunk some common legends about prophets and the prophetic. Through the debunking of falsehoods and misconceptions, there should be clarity through present-day truth and scriptural backing.

Prophets No Longer Exist

Here in the 21st century, many question the validity of prophets. Many ministries and ministers question why prophets are necessary today. They teach that the office of the prophet ended centuries ago, but have no validation of such a claim. Prophets are as needed today as in Biblical times. The claims of the non-existence of prophets came from those who have no understanding of prophets, have experienced false prophets and have not been healed or refuse to accept God's messengers.

The teachings of the non-existence of prophets usually state that since the bible was canonized, there is no longer a need for prophets. This is not true. The bible, being sixty-six books, did not cause prophets to no longer function in the earth. These kinds of teachings are dangerous to the Body of Christ at large. Where there is no vision (prophetic word, instruction, revelation from God), the people perish (Proverbs 29:18). God uses His prophets to reveal secrets and mysteries of the Kingdom of God and we as disciples and believers in Christ; we must receive whom God chooses to speak for Him.

Prophets exist today. Prophets are still speaking for God as He instructs them. Just like in the days of old, prophets are in the earth, speaking God's will and advancing His government (kingdom) and ecclesia in the earth.

Many question the existence of prophets because of the ability of believers to prophesy. The question becomes if believers can prophesy by Holy Spirit, why do we need prophets? The problem with this is, many do not understand that prophesying does not make you a prophet. Holy Spirit will use believers to prophesy, however, this is not the only function of a prophet. Prophets are needed for the advancing of the kingdom, edifying of the Body and foundation building of the universal church. The prophesying of believers and the function of prophets is needed and purposed to work together, not against each other.

We must remember, prophets are governmental officials. Governmental officials and civilians do not always have the same level of information. All believers can prophesy, but not near the level of prophets. Believers will prophesy to each other and even to ministries but they are not prophesying to governments and nations, that is reserved for government officials. Prophets prophesy from the place of God's governance and law unto individuals and nations. (Acts 3:21; First Corinthians 12:28; Ephesians 3:5; 4:11; Second Peter 3:2)

Prayer of Repentance
Father, forgive your people for questioning the validity of prophets. Continue to reveal Your purpose of prophets especially in the 21st century. Many have been hurt by those claiming to be prophets, never actually encountered a prophet or simply do not understand, make Your prophets known to the church and the world for Your glory. Forgive us in Jesus' name, amen.

Major and Minor Prophets

Some of us have been taught an erred concept of prophets. We have been taught that God has specifications that will make some major and others minor. This concept has created a competitive spirit amongst prophets. Some prophets have believed that they can obtain major status through works. Some prophets have shrunk back from moving forward as prophets because they saw themselves (through the eyes of others) as minor. God NEVER sanctioned major and minor prophets.

God's prophets are not to be against one another. People have created a flawed hierarchical view to God and those He has called into leadership. We function with a totem pole in the earth - not in Heaven. God is not a respecter of persons that He would designate one major and one minor. This concept has caused many to respect some prophets over others and even make some prophets idols.

Designating a major and minor prophet is a flawed attempt to understand the biblical books of the prophets. The thought is, the prophets with longer books are major and those with shorter books are minor. This concept is not of God and creates within certain believers a thought to not read the 'minor prophets' because the message is not as important. Every prophet is important to God and as His sons and disciples we should not classify prophets in a way that He did not.

Over the years, I have heard many people claim to be a major prophet. Scripture in no way backs this proclamation. The majority of people claiming to be a major prophet have issues with pride, narcissism and accountability. There are many who have taken an elitist mindset, believing they are major prophets. They do not believe in mutual account-ability to other prophets or to any leadership within the church. This is dangerous because all prophets have to be accountable to prevent becoming an island unto him or herself or becoming contaminated with falsehood. Not many people, as you would imagine, proclaim to be minor prophets, but their actions are a reflection of the thought. Those who think they are minor prophets act as if no one will ever receive what they have to say and usually spend a lot of time comparing their ministry to others. Those who think they are minor prophets also struggle with low self-esteem and desire to make everyone happy which can lead to compromise.

All prophets have different mantles, mandates and administration of the anointing, and none is better than the other. We have to destroy this concept and embrace God's prophets. All of the prophets within scripture did not have a known name but His word still manifested.

For there is no respect of persons with God. Romans 2:11

But if ye have respect to persons, ye commit sin, and are convinced of the law as transgressors. James 2:9

With the two verses above, we have to evaluate ourselves. Do we have a demarcation that God Himself does not have? He has NO respect of persons, so we cannot have respect of persons either. We need to repent for receiving one prophet over another.

All prophets, whether in scripture of old, or alive today, speak from the same Spirit, the Breath of God. None of God's prophet's spoke of themselves, only of Him and His purpose in the earth. The length of a book or the number of ministry engagements does not determine how God sees a prophet, nor should it for us, His people. Every prophet is needful within the grace God has purposed for him or her. All prophets are not the same and God purposed it that way.

Scripture only categorized prophets in two ways: His and holy.
1. Holy ~ Second Chronicles 20:20; 29:25: 36:16; Acts 3:18 and Romans 1:2
2. His ~ Luke 1:70; Acts 3:21; Second Peter 3:2 and Revelation 22:6

Prayer of Repentance
Father, forgive us for allowing a doctrine (teaching) created by the tradition of man to cause us to have demarcation within ourselves for Your prophets. Correct our error with Your truth that we would receive your prophets and we may encounter You through them. Forgive us and show us the right way to receive Your prophets in Jesus' name.

<u>Prophets are Mean</u>

Mean: intend to convey, indicate, or refer to (a particular thing or notion); signify: (New Oxford American Dictionary)

Mean is not defined as we have been using it. Mean is not an adjective (a word or phrase that describes a noun), it is a verb (a word of action). Mean in our understanding has been rude, nasty, inconsiderate and even unapproachable. Many prophets have been improperly labeled as mean. Some people have encountered stern or serious prophets and labeled them as mean.

Serious: (a person) solemn or thoughtful in character or manner (New Oxford American Dictionary)

Stern: (a person or their manner) serious and unrelenting, especially in the assertion of authority and exercise of discipline: (New Oxford American Dictionary)

Both serious and stern are adjectives that should apply to all prophets. Prophets have to be careful not to allow their flesh to intervene, which will cause people to mislabel them. Prophets are not God's whipping stick, they are to carry His rod, tempered in love for the building of the Body of Christ in love. If serious and stern are not met with the love of God, it will appear to be rude, nasty, inconsiderate and unapproachable. Some people, who are prophets, have done a great disservice to the Body of Christ because of an erred teaching and mindset of what they are to do with seriousness and sternness.

Being stern and serious does not mean prophets are unable to have fun. Many have been taught that prophets cannot laugh or enjoy life, which is a lie. Too often we talk about what we cannot do, failing to realize we made a decision to obey the word of God. What we consider restrictions from having a life is a decision to be in the safety of God. Prophets are to be balanced and not take personal emotions out on the people of God. Prophets are people who desire to enjoy life like other believers, a natural desire. However, prophets are to live a life dedicated to God. In living a life dedicated to God, their appetites are not like everybody else's, not willing to entertain carnality.

Prayer of Repentance

As a prophet, I want to repent to God and the people of God for our mishandling of His word, His love and His people. Lord, I stand proxy for ALL Your prophets who have missed their assignment by allowing their flesh to make them rude, nasty, inconsiderate and unapproachable. I understand prophets carry a serious assignment and we do not have the right to mistreat people in the name of the Lord or in the name of being a prophet. Temper us with Your love that our delivery of Your word will be with perfect love, casting out fear of damnation, curses and disapproval from You. Forgive us, Lord and cleanse us in Jesus' name.

Prophets Are Deep

Over the years, many people have labeled prophets as DEEP! Deep has a negative connotation attached to it. People label prophets as deep because they do not know how to handle them. Prophets are not like ordinary people. they think, speak and act differently than most people know or understand. Prophets are deep and that is not a bad thing. Prophets, as all believers should be, are deep as God is deep. God has purposely concealed Himself in levels, dimensions and realms that can only be accessed by those whom He calls.

Deep calleth unto deep at the noise of thy waterspouts: all thy waves and thy billows are gone over me. (Psalm 42:7)

The deep in God calls to the deep in us. God desires believers and prophets to come beyond the initial relationship, revelation and come deeper into Him. It is like learning to swim; you start in the shallow end and as you learn the techniques, you go deeper and deeper in the water. It is the same with God. Deep is necessary, important and expected.

Holy Spirit is leading us into wider, deeper and higher understanding of Him and His Realm, which we call Heaven. He is Knowledge and Wisdom personified and we must allow Him to lead us without carnal logic inserting itself. We have to rely on His communicating with our spirit and not trying to make our mind the focus of our obedience. We must allow Him to lead us where our faith is without limits. Too often we limit our faith in Him by allowing logic to reason His instruction and leading.

This season, and every season, we have to embrace the calling into deeper. This new place in the realm of the Spirit is your normal, but does not yet seem normal to you. It is still unknown to you, until you begin to encounter the depth, width and height of where you are. You cannot determine what is supposed to happen in this realm because you have never been here before. Holy Spirit wants to make you acquainted with Him and this realm all the more. He is calling you into a fresh place and only He knows what you are to expect, receive and encounter in this realm.

Yes, prophets are deep, as they should be. Prophets are to be a deep well of God's secrets, power and wisdom. Stop accepting the negative connotations of deep and be deep in the Lord, with the Lord and for the Lord.

<u>Prayer of Repentance</u>
Father, forgive your prophets for allowing the perception of men to cause them to be shallow. Forgive us for allowing the faces and reactions of men to cause us to fear and compromise our positions with you. Renew Your right Spirit within us and birth boldness that would allow us to speak as we ought for Your glory in Jesus' name, amen.

<u>Old Testament Prophets vs. New Testament Prophets</u>

There is much debate within prophetic circles if the prophets of the Old Testament, and New Testament prophets, are totally different. Many are teaching that the mandate of the prophet has changed. This debate has bred the current flow of false prophecy and false prophets that have recently arisen. There is not a difference in prophets of old and prophets of today. As long as we make a difference between prophets, we also segregate the voice of the Lord in the earth.

We are battling an unnecessary fight from within. The prophets of old are our brothers, we are of one prophetic linage tracing back to God Himself. We are one brotherhood, let us unify in Holy Spirit instead of separating over false interpretation of scripture. Both old and new prophets, speak from God's word and Spirit and it becomes His law. It is interesting for me to see prophets of today, claiming to have mantles and anointings of prophets of old, yet they do not do the same thing. You cannot carry the mantle of an Elijah, but believe your assignment is different than his. That would make the mantle of no effect and powerless. You cannot take the mantle of an Old Testament prophet and have a different manifestation. This is another reason that there is no separation between old and new.

Are there differences between the two? Yes. But the mandate is still the same. The prophets of old did not have the indwelling of Holy Spirit, today's prophets do. The prophets of old spoke to one nation (Israel), the prophets of today speak to all nations. The prophets of old spoke of the coming Christ; the prophets of today speak from the ascended Christ. Even with those differences, both prophets speak the mind and will of God, watch and pray, warn and correct the people of God.

Prophets do not belong to either covenant, really. Prophets belong to God and they speak directly from His mouth. There were prophets before the covenants and the law, as we know them. Adam, Abraham, Noah, just to name a few, were prophets before there was an old covenant. We have to be careful not to box in or isolate prophets to our thoughts and restrict them from God's assignment. There are no prophets of the law or prophets of grace but only prophets of God. God used prophets to establish His law and His grace.

<u>Prayer of Repentance</u>
Father, forgive us for making differences within Your prophets. We have forgotten that prophets belong to You and not to us. We cannot determine how or when they function, we can only accept those You call, send and purpose as prophets for Your glory. As we purpose to realign with Your prophetic order, structure and protocol, please give us greater understanding of true prophets and prophetics in Jesus' name, amen.

Prophets Only Confirm

One of the myths about the prophet's assignment is "all they do is confirm". Many people believe, and teach, that if a prophet says something you have not heard before, it is not of God. THIS IS NOT TRUE. As we study prophets, prophet spoke from the mouth of God and most of what they were instructed to speak was not heard before in the ears of the people. When a prophet is reduced to a confirmer, it diminishes God's true prophetic release. Prophecy is not to remind you of what God has already said to you. Prophets will remind you of what God has already accomplished. (Judges 6:8-10)

As we look at prophets like Samuel, Elijah, Obadiah even Jonah, we see that they prophesied futuristic events, warned of judgment and prepared people for God's redemptive plan, not confirmed what the people already knew. A prophet carries the message of the King and His Kingdom with the purpose of bringing alignment, positioning for destiny and proper understanding of the King's desire.

We have been taught, improperly, from scripture that two or three witnesses establish EVERY word, this is not accurate. When we actually look at the verses that are used to build this teaching, they are not about receiving or obeying the prophetic word of the Lord.

At the mouth of two witnesses, or three witnesses, shall he that is worthy of death be put to death; but at the mouth of one witness he shall not be put to death. (Deuteronomy 17:6)

One witness shall not rise up against a man for any iniquity, or for any sin, in any sin that he sinneth: at the mouth of two witnesses, or at the mouth of three witnesses, shall the matter be established. (Deuteronomy 19:15)

Against an elder receive not an accusation, but before two or three witnesses. (1 Timothy 5:19)

None of these verses deal with receiving a prophetic word. God speaks and God uses prophets to speak, you have to choose whether you will obey or not. If God uses a prophet to confirm what He said, it is because you have not obeyed what He already instructed you to do. Confirmation is not the best thing to have when you have heard God. After hearing God, obey Him and stop looking for signs and confirmations.

Then certain of the scribes and of the Pharisees answered, saying, Master, we would see a sign from thee. But he answered and said unto them, An evil and adulterous generation seeketh after a sign; and there shall no sign be given to it, but the sign of the prophet Jonas: For as Jonas was three days and three nights in the whale's belly; so shall the Son of man be three days and three nights in the heart of the earth. (Matthew 12:38-40)

Jesus is teaching about his crucifixion, which is to come. The people are asking for a sign, though there are hundreds, maybe thousands, of prophetic words foretelling of his death. As Jesus is addressing the request for a sign, he calls the people, evil and adulterous. Why are the people evil and adulterous? Because they are not receiving by faith and are stepping outside of their covenant with God looking for temporal signs and confirmations. Jesus is teaching and prophesying about what will happen and the people want confirmation, literally telling Jesus your word is not enough, prove it.

These are functions of the prophets:

1. <u>Pray</u>

Before a prophet can prophesy to the people, they must learn and mature in communication with God; through prayer. No prophet of God can function without prayer; it is his or her breath.

Abram (later renamed Abraham) is affirmed a prophet by the voice of God to the king. No other person had been called a prophet yet in scripture. What does the Lord say the prophet will do? PRAY! Prophets spend many hours in prayer. Prayer is the lifeline to the prophetic. When prayer is removed from the prophetic, it becomes tainted and impure. Prayer will keep righteousness and holiness before the prophet as they stay before the Lord. (Genesis 20)

The prophet-priest, Jeremiah, tells the people "I hear what you are saying. I will take it to the Lord in prayer and I will tell you whatever He says. I will not hide or keep anything from you as He speaks". Many times, people will come to the prophet with an idea of what they want to hear as an answer to their struggles, supplications, etc. but they are not open to what God will say. Jeremiah clearly tells the people; I will only speak what He says. Prophets can only speak what the Lord is speaking to them, not their opinion, not their assumption - but what is spoken by the voice of the prophetic. Prophets, remember there is one voice, you repeat what He has spoken. Do not try to become a wonder without Him who is wonderful. Speak as He speaks, release His voice. (Jeremiah 42)

The depth of your prayer life determines the depth of your flow in the prophetic! Prophets, the more you are engaged in prayer, the more sensitive you are to Holy Spirit and desensitized to the world. *Prophets*, your life of prayer should mature into an unending conversation with the Lord. Continue to grow and mature in prayer, develop an intimate language and a love for prayer.

2. <u>Intercede</u>
But if they be prophets, and if the word of the LORD be with them, let them now make intercession to the LORD of hosts, that the vessels which are left in the house of the

LORD, and in the house of the king of Judah, and at Jerusalem, go not to Babylon. (Jeremiah 27:18)

Prophets are called to intercession as much as they are called to pray. The things God reveals can be affected by intercession. Intercession brings the prophet to the council table with God. The prophet steps out of the place of the spokesperson for God and becomes judge with God.

Abraham interceded after the Lord revealed His plan to destroy Sodom and Gomorrah. His intercession kept the plan of God from happening immediately. Abraham's intercession did not manifest into repentance of the people, however his intercession did allow him to rescue Lot's family.

3. <u>Deliver and Preserve</u>
    And by a prophet the LORD brought (delivered) Israel out of Egypt, and by a prophet was he preserved.
    (Hosea 12:13)

The Israelites were delivered by the prophet Moses and preserved by him as well. When a prophet is used to bring deliverance, it is by divine instruction and providence. Moses had specific instructions on how to deliver the Israelites from the Egyptian's bondage. After their deliverance, he was given specific instructions to preserve them until they reached the promise land (prophesied place).

Preserve comes from the Hebrew word *shamar*. *Shamar* is transliterated as keep/keeper, watchman, save and guard/protect. The prophet is used as God's guard of holiness, righteousness and law (command, instruction). Prophets are used in deliverance to bring people out and up from circumstances, situations and sins that displease God.

4. <u>Revive</u>
And the LORD heard the voice of Elijah; and the soul of the child came into him again, and he revived. (1 Kings 17:22)

The ministry of prophets is one that will bring dead men back to life. Through prophesying and the other functions of prophets, we can be revived and given life. The children of Israel were dead through their years of bondage, so God raised a prophet to revive them. The children of Israel had a slave mentality, but they had to be revived to the spiritual reality that their destiny was to be a kingdom of priests.

And it came to pass, as they were burying a man, that, behold, they spied a band of men; and they cast the man into the sepulchre of Elisha: and when the man was let down, and touched the bones of Elisha, he revived, and stood up on his feet. (2 Kings 13:21)

Even in death, Elisha was still reviving people. Reviving is another form of deliverance. The life and ministry of God's prophets are used to revive the people of God. Revival is a mandate of the prophet's function. They are carriers of the Life of God to the people of God. Speaking the reality of God's thoughts about His people will revive them after years of identity confusion and frustration.

5. <u>Remind</u>
That the LORD sent a prophet unto the children of Israel, which said unto them, Thus saith the LORD God of Israel, I brought you up from Egypt, and brought you forth out of the house of bondage; And I delivered you out of the hand of the Egyptians, and out of the hand of all that oppressed you, and drave them out from before you, and gave you their land; And I said unto you, I am the LORD your God; fear not the gods of the Amorites, in whose land ye dwell:

but ye have not obeyed my voice. (Judges 6:8-10)

God will use His prophets to remind His people what He has done for them. Sometimes, especially between generations, people forget what has already transpired and how God has delivered. They have to be reminded. A reminder will cause us to think and thank. Sometimes, we need a flashback to keep us humbled and grateful for all that God has done and provided. He will remind us of what He has done as He is preparing us for more.

6. <u>Prophesy</u>
Prophesying is inclusive of giving instruction, foretelling and revealing.

But he that prophesieth speaketh unto men to edification, and exhortation, and comfort. He that speaketh in an unknown tongue edifieth himself; but he that prophesieth edifieth the church. (1 Corinthians 14:3-4)

a. <u>Edification</u> comes from the Greek word, *oikodomē* which means: the act of one who promotes another's growth in Christian wisdom, piety, happiness, holiness
b. <u>Exhortation</u> comes from the Greek word, *paraklēsis which means:* importation, supplication, entreaty, admonition, encouragement, consolation, comfort, solace; that which affords comfort or refreshment, instructive and powerful hortatory discourse.
c. <u>Comfort</u> comes from the Greek word, *paramythia* which means any address, whether made for the purpose of persuading, or of arousing and stimulating, or of calming and consoling.

What Does Prophecy Do?
1. <u>Prophecy Foretells</u> (Prediction)

Yea, and all the prophets from Samuel and those that follow after, as many as have spoken, have likewise foretold of these days. Ye are the children of the prophets, and of the covenant which God made with our fathers, saying unto Abraham, And in thy seed shall all the kindreds of the earth be blessed. (Acts 3:24-25)

One aspect of prophecy is foretelling or telling an event beforehand. Prophets foretell the future as God sees it, not as the prophet sees it. Many of the prophets of old prophesied of the coming Christ. Prophecy can be short-range or long-range in the scope of its delivery. Isaiah prophesied about the new heavens and earth that John saw in revelation, thousands of years beforehand.

2. <u>Prophecy Instructs</u>
Prophecy will instruct you on how to handle a situation. God uses prophecy to prepare us for times and seasons in the earth. As God is the Master Strategist, he also gives us instructional strategy to overcome, subdue and occupy until He comes.

Now there cried a certain woman of the wives of the sons of the prophets unto Elisha, saying, Thy servant my husband is dead; and thou knowest that thy servant did fear the Lord: and the creditor is come to take unto him my two sons to be bondmen. And Elisha said unto her, What shall I do for thee? tell me, what hast thou in the house? And she said, Thine handmaid hath not any thing in the house, save a pot of oil. Then he said, Go, borrow thee vessels abroad of all thy neighbours, even empty vessels; borrow not a few. And when thou art come in, thou shalt shut the door upon thee and upon thy sons, and shalt pour out into all those vessels, and thou shalt set aside that which is full. So she went from him, and shut the door upon her and upon her sons, who brought the vessels to her; and she poured out.

And it came to pass, when the vessels were full, that she said unto her son, Bring me yet a vessel. And he said unto her, There is not a vessel more. And the oil stayed. Then she came and told the man of God. And he said, Go, sell the oil, and pay thy debt, and live thou and thy children of the rest. (2 Kings 4:1-7)

Elisha is used to prophetically instruct a burdened widow and her sons concerning their debt. Elisha asked what is in the house. The mother needed strategy (instruction) so her sons would not become slaves (bondsmen). Elisha begins to prophesy from the business mind of God. He told the woman and her sons to get investors (borrow vessels), go into their home and close the door behind them. They are instructed to take the vial of oil and pour it into the vessels that were borrowed. After completing the first set of instructions, they return to Elisha and he instructs them further. The instructions of Elisha: take care of their debt and allow them to have more leftover; prophecy will open you to the overflow of God.

Jesus prophetically instructs the disciples on many occasions. He prophetically instructs them to go to the water, catch a fish and pay their taxes with the money in the mouth of the fish. Jesus prophetically instructs Peter that when he is converted, to strengthen his brothers after revealing the plot of the enemy. Prophetic instruction is necessary in guiding men through this process.

3. <u>Prophecy Reveals</u>
Surely the Lord GOD will do nothing, but he revealeth his secret unto his servants the prophets. (Amos 3:7)

God is never without a witness in the earth. He will tell His prophets His secrets and counsel before He does it in the earth. God is accountable for His actions as much as we are. He reveals His plans for judgment, restoration, redemption and His new things in the earth. The prophets are to carry God's secrets until He instructs them to speak. Through the bible, prophets are used to speak God's plan that man has no natural idea of.

God reveals His secrets to those He can trust. Everything is not put in the hands of everyone. As prophets, and believers mature, God will grant them great revelation of Him, His kingdom and His word. God always uses prophets to reveal His character, the hearts of men and future events. He uses revelation of prophets to correct, rebuke and prepare His people.

4. <u>Prophecy Warns</u>
And Jonah began to enter into the city a day's journey, and he cried, and said, Yet forty days, and Nineveh shall be overthrown. (Jonah 3:4)

So thou, O son of man, I have set thee a watchman unto the house of Israel; therefore thou shalt hear the word at my mouth, and warn them from me. (Ezekiel 33:7)

Warn comes from the Hebrew word, *zahar. Zahar is transliterated* to enlighten (by caution): admonish, shine, teach, (give) warn(-ing).

The prophet hears God's word and warns (and prepares) the people about what is coming. All warning is not of danger coming; it can also be of good coming as well. The warning function of prophecy will teach the receiver how to handle their current and even future situations.

Prophets, no matter how prophetic you are, YOU DO NOT KNOW IT ALL! Do not feel guilt or shame when something happens and you have no revelation of it. God does have other prophets that He speaks to; you only have a part of His entire revelation. You are not a know-it-all, you are a prophet.

7. <u>Be Examples</u>
Take, my brethren, the prophets, who have spoken in the name of the Lord, for an example of suffering affliction, and of patience. (James 5:10)

Prophets are to be examples to the Body of Christ. They are standard bearers in the Kingdom of God.

a. Suffering affliction, comes from the Greek word, *kakopatheia which means* hardship:—suffering affliction.

Many are the afflictions of the righteous: but the LORD delivereth him out of them all. (Psalm 34:19)

Thou therefore endure hardness, as a good soldier of Jesus Christ. (2 Timothy 2:3)

Prophets are examples of going and coming through afflictions and hardship. As standard bearers, they show the body how to overcome any and all negativity.

b. Patience comes from the Greek word, *makrothymia. Makrothymia is transliterated* patience, forbearance, longsuffering, slowness in avenging wrongs, endurance and constancy.

As examples of patience, prophets have to be longsuffering and constancy in their stance for the Kingdom and in what they experience. Prophets endure many things and cannot rely on their flesh or carnal responses.

<u>Prayer of Repentance</u>:

Father, we come asking that you forgive us for demanding signs and confirmations to believe You and Your word. We purpose to walk in faith that comes from Your word and not look for temporal signs for an eternal manifestation. We do not want to be evil and adulterous in Your eyes, as we surrender to Your will, continue to reveal Your word that we would have a pure, holy and strong faith in You!

<u>Doom and Gloom</u>

In this new age of prophetics, many condemn the prophets of old as prophets of doom and gloom. This label is a disgrace to prophets who are called, ordained and used to prophesy and release God's mind into the earth and world. God is not a powder puff, speaking what man wants to hear; man looks for prosperity in materialistic things and a constant stay of happiness (which is momentary). God has, and will, use prophets to pronounce and execute His judgment in the earth. God has not stopped releasing His mind against that which does not line up with His word. All judgment is not death or destruction as many see it. As a righteous Judge, God uses His prophets to release words of judgment, reconciliation and restoration. Doom and gloom is man's failed attempt at trying to facilitate God's word in their own wisdom.

But if they be prophets, and if the word of the Lord be with them, let them now make intercession to the Lord of hosts, that the vessels which are left in the house of the Lord, and in the house of the king of Judah, and at Jerusalem, go not to Babylon. (Jeremiah 27:18)

After God has spoken a word of judgment, it is the responsibility of the prophet to intercede, not boast in the word or the fact that God used them. They must intercede for the people and pray that they align with God. The intercession of a prophet can cause a people to repent (turn away from wickedness and turn to God), which can cause God to change His mind about the situation.

Along with the doom and gloom theology has come a doctrine of prophets of judgment. This is also in error. No prophet has ever been assigned only to release or speak judgment. God does not speak in judgment nonstop nor should His prophets. Prophets are not allowed to speak of themselves but only of God who sent them. you are not a prophet of judgment. God speaks concerning every area of our lives and society, He is never only speaking judgment.

On the other end of the spectrum, is the errant teaching of "prosperity prophets" or those who only teach a "prosperity gospel". These prophets spend most of their time drawing men and women into giving exorbitant seeds and promise constant blessing of financial gain without righteous living or obedience. God takes pleasure in our prosperity (Psalm 35:27) however; He requires our obedience to Him in all things. Prosperity Prophets create catchy clichés that pull on emotionalism and sensationalism, but do not deposit into the soul and spirit what will allow men and women to live obedient lives to God. God, in His infinite wisdom, is not blessing any person who is not obedient to Him.

Again, God never speaks one way only. He is speaking based upon the obedience or disobedience of His creation, His people. Prophets, as God's communication ambassadors, do not speak of their own opinion or their own will, so when God is not speaking neither should the prophets. Prophets are not of judgment or prosperity, but should be of God only.

Prayer of Repentance

Father, forgive those who have taken glory in causing people to fear with doom and gloom prophecies. Restore unto the earth prophets who will intercede for Your people and not rejoice in pending judgment. Deal with and deliver many from the philosophies of judgment only or prosperity only and bring forth the truth of Your prophetic reality, information, structure and manifestation. Restore unto the vessels of Your divine knowledge and revelation, the purity, integrity and balance of Your Word (written, spoken, illustrated). Heal the church from the destructive extremes of vain philosophies and restore Your prophets to Your house, church and purpose in Jesus' name.

Hit and Miss Prophesying

Many have embraced the thought of hitting and missing concerning prophecy. This means that prophets can be accurate sometimes and inaccurate at other times. This is error, this is false and this is destroying many lives. Prophets are never to miss when it comes to prophecy. Prophets are not speaking from their knowledge or wisdom, they are to echo the voice of God. God is always right because He knows everything. How can prophets get it wrong, or miss it, if they are echoing what God has said?

When a prophet speaketh in the name of the Lord, if the thing follow not, nor come to pass, that is the thing which the Lord hath not spoken, but the prophet hath spoken it presumptuously: thou shalt not be afraid of him. (Deuteronomy 18:22)

Presumptuously comes from the Hebrew word, "zadown" which is transliterated to mean pride, arrogance and the haughtiness of heart. When prophets are not speaking words that manifest according to scripture they have not spoken of God. They have spoken from their heart, or flesh, and God does not have to fulfill it. Prophets should never miss because God, Jesus and Holy Spirit can never miss.

Prophecy is not just some words, prophecy is the truth of God's plan of future events, aligning and affirming destiny and the answer to prayers. All prophets and prophetic people need to be delivered from the teaching of hitting and missing because a false, erred or wrong prophecy can destroy people's lives. True prophecy will draw men to God, false prophecy will draw men to the prophet.

We have also a more sure word of prophecy; whereunto ye do well that ye take heed, as unto a light that shineth in a dark place, until the day dawn, and the day star arise in your hearts: Knowing this first, that no prophecy of the scripture is of any private interpretation. For the prophecy came not in old time by the will of man: but holy men of God spake as they were moved by the Holy Ghost.
(2 Peter 1:19-21)

a. 2 Peter 1:19 – Prophecy comes from *prophētikos which means pertain and proceeding from a prophet; prophetic.*
b. 2 Peter 1:20-21 – *Prophecy comes prophēteia which means* a discourse emanating from divine inspiration and declaring the purposes of God, whether by reproving and admonishing the wicked, or comforting the afflicted, or revealing things hidden; esp. by foretelling future events.

Prophecy is no joke. Those who have been graced to prophesy, prophets or those with the gifts of prophecy, should not take it lightly nor believe they can hit and miss it concerning hearing the voice of God.

To believe in hit and miss prophecy is to deny Holy

Spirit as Spirit of Truth. Truth can never lie, NEVER. We must realize that as long as we repeat exactly what is spoken, the prophecy will be accurate. Too often people insert flesh and that is when prophecy becomes erred. The prophets from Genesis to Malachi, did not have the infilling of Holy Spirit and never missed in releasing a prophetic word, how much more such those prophesying today be in tune to prophesy properly. Prophecy belongs to God and He knows the exact words for every person and situation. Too often prophets and prophesiers have tried to alter the word as they see fit, which is out of order. We do not have authority to alter prophecy in anyway because it does not belong to us. Prophets and prophesiers are only delivery people getting the word from the Spirit realm to the earth (people).

Prayer of Repentance:
Father, as a prophet, I stand and repent for those who have taught and embraced the false teaching of "hitting and missing". Bring us back to the reality of true prophecy! Realign us with Your purpose of prophecy and the effectiveness of Your delivered word to all men. We will no longer accept presumptuous prophecy but will judge all prophecy according to Your word and Your Spirit. In Jesus' Name, Amen!

Prophets are Autonomous

Another errant teaching in the 21st century is that prophets are *autonomous.* Autonomous is defined *has having the right or power to self-govern.* This is not true of prophets at all. This type of teaching causes many prophets and prophetic people to take on an "elitist" mindset. Autonomy causes prophets to be separate from the Body of Christ and creates lawless prophetics. As long as prophets attempt to be autonomous, they will be vessels of anarchy. God never called for prophets to be outside of fellowship, outside of the Body or islands unto themselves. This erroneous teaching causes rebellion and a lack of vision within the church.

Prophets do not have the right or power to self-govern whatsoever. His word, His law, His kingdom and His leaders govern God's prophets, not standing of their own accord. No prophet is ever allowed to speak outside of God's instruction. Prophets are ambassadors of God's kingdom, so they echo His opinion throughout the land.

Prophets need to be a part of fellowships that will hold them accountable and will sharpen them. They can lose focus quickly and if they are not accountable; it is possible for them to cross spiritual lines. Fellowship, continued teaching and accountability will keep prophets sharp and in-tune with God. Fellowship and accountability will not substitute for personal devotion, but it will assist in the fulfilling of their prophethood.

The erred teaching that prophets are "loners" has caused much confusion. God has always worked in the dynamics of family, kingdom and team. He never sends anyone to fulfill their call alone. Not even God has worked alone in the earth that is why He created man. God and Adam worked together in the garden, God created and Adam named, that is teamwork. When God was ready to leave earth in the hands of man, he did not leave him alone; he received a helpmeet, a teammate. So, prophets are not exempt from working with others. They are not allowed to be separate from the Body and speak to the Body at the same time. If you cut off your arm, the arm is still yours but it does not function with your body anymore. It is time for the prophets, who represent the eyes, ears and mouth of God, to be fully reconnected to the Body and work fully in His ecclesia.

<u>Prayer for Repentance</u>

Father, forgive Your authentic prophets that have attempted to govern themselves instead of being a part of the household of faith. Many have isolated themselves because of fear or rejection that has never been healed. Heal the trauma and drama of Your prophets so they do not run to caves or under trees looking for the end because of unresolved issues. Reestablish Your prophets in the household of faith, Your family and Your kingdom, in Jesus's name, amen.

Samuel was a miracle baby, born from prayer and a vow to the Lord.

Chapter Two:

The Biography of Samuel

Samuel is a special kind of prophet. He is one of very few prophets whose entire life is seen throughout scripture. Samuel's birth is miraculous and his life prophetic in nature. From his conception to his death, Samuel was molded for prophetic fulfillment.

Samuel's Family

Elknah was a husband of two wives. One who was producing children (Peninnah) and one with a shut womb (Hannah). Hannah was mocked and mistreated, by his other wife, because she bore Elkanah no children. Being barren was seen as a curse during this time, however Hannah was not barren. God shut up her womb. What is the difference? A barren woman may never have a child(ren) because of some type of medical/health reasons. God shut up Hannah's womb, that she would be processed to carry God's prophet. She could not give birth before time but God's plan was strategic in birthing His reforming prophet, Samuel.

In Hannah's processing, she becomes a woman of

prayer. She pressed into GOD beyond what most people could even imagine. In the midst of praying Hannah made a vow unto the Lord:

And she vowed a vow, and said, O LORD of hosts, if thou wilt indeed look on the affliction of thine handmaid, and remember me, and not forget thine handmaid, but wilt give unto thine handmaid a man child, then I will give him unto the LORD all the days of his life, and there shall no razor come upon his head. (1 Samuel 1:11)

A part of the vow that Hannah made was that Samuel was to be a Nazarite (Numbers 6:2; 21). A Nazarite was a man or woman who purposely vowed to consecrate themselves unto the Lord by not doing certain things (Numbers 6:1-8).

After Hannah made the vow unto the Lord, she began to pray in a more intimate way. She was no longer in a place for sound to come out of her mouth but she was praying in her heart (Spirit). Samuel was a miracle baby born from prayer and a vow to the Lord. Samuel's conception being miraculous is similar to the miraculous conception of Christ. Hannah conceived Samuel in the Spirit before in the natural. Mary, the mother of Jesus, was overshadowed by Holy Spirit to conceive, what a foreshadow.

After Samuel's birth, Hannah purposed to wean him before fulfilling her vow unto the Lord. The weaning process in Hebraic culture was from 18 months to 5 years of age (from my research). Hannah refused to offer Samuel as long as he had a dependence upon her. She wanted to offer him to God free of dependence of his mother's milk that he would be able to ingest, digest and receive the word of the Lord.

As we look at the birthing of Samuel, God's prophet, we see that His lineage is one of sacrifice, prayer and faith that is radical. Samuel was no ordinary prophet because he had no ordinary conception or natural birthing.

Samuel as a Father

Samuel is a father of two sons, Joel and Abiah. As Samuel is a father, it is easy to say that he is also a husband. His wife is not mentioned; however, it was not common practice for men of Hebraic roots to have children outside the covenant of marriage. His sons, sadly, did not follow in the lineage of their father and became known for going after lucre, taking bribes and making perverse judgments.

Birthing as a Prophet

Before Samuel was birthed as a prophet, he was ministering as a servant (1 Samuel 2:11,18). He was trained in the ways of the Lord as an apprentice to Eli. Because Samuel was a young child when he served, he was wrapped in a linen ephod. A linen ephod was a priestly garment also known as a mantle. Samuel was mantled as a priest before he was birthed as a prophet. He learned how to orchestrate and maintain things of God before he was used to speak for God. This is important for budding and emerging prophets, learn the ways of God and then let Him send you.

Samuel laid next to the ark of God to sleep. What a place to sleep, literally next to the Glory of God. As he was sleeping, the LORD called out to him. Because Samuel didn't know it was the voice of the Lord, he ran to his teacher, Eli. This happened 3 times because Samuel did not know the Lord, nor was the word of the Lord revealed to him. After the Lord called Samuel 3 times, Eli instructed

Samuel how to handle hearing the Lord, He came and stood with Samuel. After the calling of the Lord and standing with the Lord, Samuel began to hear God's word against the house of Eli (his teacher), (1 Samuel 3:11-14). After Samuel's personal encounter with the Lord, he feared telling Eli what was revealed to him. Eli insisted that Samuel tell him what the Lord said. This insistence helped garner a greater level of obedience for the young Samuel. Samuel spoke as God had revealed and Eli agreed that the Lord had spoken.

Samuel's birth as a prophet was also birthing as a reformer. God used Samuel many times to bring the reformation to the children of Israel. A reformer is one used of God to usher in God's new thing in the earth. Samuel's birth as a prophet was a new thing in the earth as he is the first prophet to be trained in the priesthood and prophethood simultaneously. Samuel's prophetic birth was the reforming of the priesthood that Eli allowed to be perverted and without confrontation.

Samuel's Ministry

The Lord established Samuel as a prophet in Israel and his prophethood was known all over the land. God revealed Himself to Samuel at Shiloh; it became a consecrated place for Samuel and God. Prophets can be given particular places of revelation and intimacy with God, Shiloh was that place for Samuel.

After Samuel's birthing as a prophet, Israel experienced a lot of warfare, the loss of the Ark of the Covenant, even the death of all of the male leaders in the house of Eli. The reemergence of Samuel comes in with a word of repentance (1 Samuel 7:3).

Samuel is not prophesying about their sin but their redemption. All they have to do is repent, turn away from the sin that has been committed. After repentance, there are instructions that must be fulfilled to see God's deliverance. God is not always using prophets to whip the people for their sins. His will is that all come unto repentance (2 Peter 3:9). No prophet is allowed to only speak of the sins and unfaithfulness of the people without speaking about the opportunity to repent and return to God.

Judge

Judges ruled Israel and Samuel was a judge. Samuel is not only a prophet of God, he is also used in the realm (mountain, sphere) of government. As a judge, he is the highest-ranking official in the land. As a prophet and judge, Samuel is expected to make righteous judgments and execute the law of God in the land. There are fifteen known judges of Israel. Fourteen men and one woman served as judges over Israel.

Samuel serving as a judge allowed him to also serve in intercession. Being born of a woman of prayer and sacrifice, Samuel took on her mantle and began to function as one interceding and sacrificing for Israel. Through his intercession and sacrificing, the Philistines that fought Israel were subdued. All the cities they possessed from Israel were restored and there was peace between Israel and the Amorites. Samuel judged from his home in Ramah and judged all the days of his life.

Anointer

Samuel's sons were corrupt and the children of Israel asked for a king to reign over them. Again, Samuel is used to reform and bring in a new season for the people of God. As the children of Israel had never had a king, Samuel was instrumental in the transition from judges to kings. God commissions Samuel to reform the leadership structure of Israel and to anoint the first king, Saul. Saul was God's choice, revealed to Samuel through speaking in his ear.

Many times, we are taught that the children of Israel begged for a king. However, in scripture, we see that they requested a king because there were no integral judges in the land. They only asked once and God granted the request because they were rejecting His reign over them. We, as a people have to be very careful that we are not requesting anything that would reject God's reign over us.

Saul's kingship started off well but ended in destruction. Saul rebelled against the instructions of God and God rejected him while allowing him to train his replacement. Saul was a warrior but he was prideful and disobedient. Samuel was commissioned again to anoint another king. But first he was rebuked for his perception of what the king should look like. The great prophet was not discerning God's choice. He thought the next king would not look like Saul. God deals with His prophets concerning their perception to keep them in alignment with Him.

The next king of Israel chosen by God was David. David was the youngest son of Jesse. He served as the shepherd of his father's sheep. David wrestled a lion and bear to protect his father's sheep. With the confidence of overcoming the lion and bear, he then overcame Goliath, a giant Philistine who was harassing the children of Israel. Samuel was commissioned to anoint the second king of Israel as well.

As an anointer, Samuel's assignment was to smear oil upon the new kings. The oil represents the anointing of God. Both Saul and David had to be anointed because they were to rule in the anointing of God. Samuel, the reforming prophet is used to anoint the markers of God's new thing in the earth.

As an anointer, Samuel was also utilized by God to ordain and set people in office. David and Samuel ordained two hundred and twelve porters (gatekeepers). They ordained them and set them in four wards to oversee the gates of the house of God (1 Chronicles 9).

Teacher & Writer

Israel never had kings before, so Samuel received two assignments: write and teach about the kingdom. Samuel was charged to explain to Israel the ordinances, processes and procedures, and their rights, customs and privileges within this new way of leading them. After he taught the people, he wrote a book of the manner of the king and presented it to God by laying it before Him.

Overseer

David is on the run from Saul who is trying to kill him. He runs right to Samuel's house in Ramah. David and Samuel then go dwell in Naioth. Naioth is a dwelling place for prophets in Ramah. Saul found out where David was and sent men to capture him but they saw the prophets prophesying and Samuel was overseeing the prophesying. Again, prophetic team ministry, this is not a 21st century concept; this has happened throughout scripture. Samuel is referenced as overseeing or being the overseer of the prophets prophesying.

Despite what many think, prophecy should be watched by a senior leader. Samuel, being a senior prophet, is the best example of overseeing prophets and prophesying. Saul sent messengers three times and all of them began to prophesy under the spirit of prophecy that was released in the gathering of prophets. These men did not become prophets but because of the spirit of God, they prophesied. Saul travels to Ramah himself and the Spirit of God is so thick and heavy that he prophesies until he gets to Naioth. Saul strips naked and prophesies before Samuel, laying all day and night. With all the prophesying Saul did, he was not a prophet - just operating with the Spirit of God.

Samuel's Death

Samuel died and all of Israel lamented. He was buried in his house in Ramah, the place from where he judged Israel. Saul becomes afraid of the Philistines and inquires of the Lord, but the Lord is not responding. Saul requested that a woman with a familiar spirit be found. Saul allowed his impatience to cause him to seek answers from an impure place. God had already commanded any man or woman with a familiar spirit be put to death by stoning yet Saul is looking to get answers from this familiar spirit.

Saul knows something is wrong with what he is doing. When he travels to the woman with the familiar spirit, he disguises himself and speaks almost in riddles. He is not straightforward with what he is doing, that is a sign he knew it was wrong to do. The woman challenges Saul about seeking her out because of the law of the land. Saul promises the woman that no punishment would come to her.

The woman asked Saul whom he wanted her to bring up. When he says Samuel, she exposes that it was Saul before her. Saul tells her to not be afraid of what she has seen. She reveals she sees gods ascending out of the earth and an old man with a mantle. Saul perceives that the old man with the mantle was Samuel.

Samuel asked Saul why he disquieted (perturb, agitate)

him to bring him up. Saul explains that he is fearful of the Philistines and does not know what to do because the Lord has not answered him. Samuel delivered a strong word about Saul's disobedience to God and how the Philistines were going to take Israel and that Saul and his sons were going to die. The word that was delivered unto Saul came to pass. (1 Samuel 31)

Saul visiting the woman with a familiar spirit is controversial. Many debate whether it was Samuel or not. I have questioned it as well. Samuel is definitely dead, however what Saul perceived to be Samuel prophesied an accurate word to him. Does this prove it was Samuel? Not necessarily. Saul was in a prideful and rejected state; his perception was skewed at best. This part of Samuel's death will always be controversial; however, his life is still a rarity and worth knowing about.

Isaiah's ministry and life is an interesting view of prophetic range. His range of ministry and prophetic vision, hearing and manifestation are almost unparalleled.

Chapter Three:

The Biography of Isaiah

Isaiah's ability to prophesy beyond current season to seasons that he would not personally see, is amazing. The prophecy of Isaiah is referred to as the "mini bible" as it has sixty-six chapters and our bible has sixty-six books.

Isaiah's Family

Through scripture, Isaiah is connected to his father. Verses will mention Isaiah and his father, Amoz. It is interesting, as much as Isaiah's father is mentioned in scripture, his mother is not. Not much is known of Isaiah's early life but we do see his spiritual birthing and mantling.

Isaiah was a man of covenant as he was a husband. Isaiah was also a father. Prophetess, Isaiah's wife, is unnamed but she is referenced for a reason. She has purpose even without us knowing her name. Isaiah and his wife have two sons, Shearjashub and Mahershalalhashbaz.

Behold, I and the children whom the LORD hath given me are for signs and for wonders in Israel from the LORD of hosts, which dwelleth in mount Zion. (Isaiah 8:18)

The aforementioned scripture declares that Isaiah and his children are to be signs and wonders in Israel. That is a powerful expression of God's purpose for a family. This speaks to families working together in life and ministry to present God's view of how family works. All children born to ministers are not going to be what the world, and even some of the church, deem them to be. Before there was a kingdom, a church, ministry, there was family and family can do ministry together for the glory of God.

Isaiah's Spiritual Birthing

Isaiah had a supernatural encountering with the Lord and with Heaven. After King Uzziah died, Isaiah was brought into a spiritual place he had not encountered before. Isaiah had already been functioning as a prophet before Uzziah died, somehow, it is like Uzziah's death became a seed for Isaiah's supernatural encounter.

Break Down of Isaiah's Encounter

"I saw also the Lord sitting upon a throne, high and lifted up" – recognizing that the Lord is King. Isaiah saw Him from His place of rulership and majesty. This is when Isaiah encounters and understands the Lord as the highly-exalted God. The Most High God, El Elyon, He who is sovereign over all, is now revealing Himself to Isaiah. Isaiah is in the presence of sovereignty!

"and his train filled the temple" – The train of a king's robe represents how many kingdoms he has subdued and conquered. The train of the Lord's, filling His temple (holy place; sanctuary) shows that no kingdom has power over God in any way; He is the conqueror of all kingdoms of the earth (Revelation 11:15).

After encountering God, Isaiah begins to encounter God's atmosphere. God is constantly amongst angels and now so is Isaiah. As Isaiah is encountering Heaven and the angels, he is brought into their worship. He hears their songs and crying out about the Lord. He is very similar to what Apostle John encountered in the Spirit while on the Isle of Patmos (Isaiah 6:3; Revelation 4:8)

As Isaiah is encountering this spiritual awakening, he realizes that his flesh is not good. That he is also among people who are undone or incomplete. He realizes that after seeing the KING. He realizes there is more to life, there is more to his walk with the Lord. With the revelation of being undone, incomplete, God allows an angel to get a live (hot) coal from the altar to lay upon Isaiah's lips. The live coal from the altar was used to purge Isaiah for his assignment. I would venture to say that coal came from the brazen altar, the place of sacrifice. Isaiah was being birthed into a greater place in his prophethood. Interesting, after Isaiah was purged, he heard the Lord. Deliverance will give you open access to the mouth of God. Deliverance will also cause you to have confidence to go where God needs a person to stand for Him.

Isaiah was already in full time ministry when this spiritual awakening happened. He already had visions about Judah and Jerusalem and was already speaking for the Lord. Isaiah's spiritual awakening after the death of Uzziah represents that prophets are constantly being brought into deeper levels of God. The spiritual awakening brought deliverance to the Lord. Deliverance will open you to the voice of the Lord more than ever before. This time in the presence and inhabitation of God causes Isaiah to want to do anything the Lord needed done and opened his willingness to go and do the will of God.

Isaiah's Mantling

Isaiah functioned in many prophetic streams. He was utilized by God in a multifaceted way of prophesying and fulfilling his prophetic assignment in the earth.

Isaiah is the prophet quoted most often in the New Testament. The Book of Isaiah is second only to Psalms in the number of verse quotations found in the New Testament. The Book of Isaiah is a collection of poetic prophecy, generally divided into the Book of Judgment (Chapters 1-39) and the Book of Consolation (Chapters 40-66).

Ministry Timespan

Isaiah was the prophet during the reign of 4 kings spanning 113 years.

>Uzziah reigned 52 years
>Jotham reigned 16 years
>Azah reigned 16 years
>Hezekiah reigned 29 years

Isaiah had one of the longest prophethoods within scripture. His prophethood was not only long in the extent of his service, but also his prophecies. Isaiah prophesied about the coming Christ, the new heaven and the earth (Isaiah 65:17; 66:22) and even about Lucifer (Isaiah 14). Isaiah's ministry was not restricted to time but functioned from eternity. Isaiah was able to reveal things of old, things current and things to come.

Isaiah Discusses Lucifer

Earlier it was mentioned that Isaiah prophesied about Lucifer. Lucifer is not mentioned in scripture anywhere, except the one mention in the book of Isaiah. No other prophet is given the revelation of how Lucifer attempted to overthrow the throne of God.

Isaiah 14:12-15
How art thou fallen from heaven, O Lucifer, son of the morning! how art thou cut down to the ground, which didst weaken the nations! For thou hast said in thine heart, I will ascend into heaven, I will exalt my throne above the stars of God: I will sit also upon the mount of the congregation, in the sides of the north: I will ascend above the heights of the clouds; I will be like the most High. Yet thou shalt be brought down to hell, to the sides of the pit.

Isaiah's ministry is one that surpasses time and speaks in all three dimensions of time: past; present and future.

Isaiah's Prophetic Functions

Visionary

Isaiah was a visionary prophet meaning he saw a lot in the Spirit. He was used to prophesy what he saw. The seer stream of the prophetic can be controversial because, it too, is misunderstood. One who is allowed to see into the spirit realm whether by dream, vision or trance, is as much a prophet as one who hears the voice of the Lord (1 Samuel 9:9). God allows seers into His will by visual revelation and prophetic showings or pictures.

Audio (Hearing the Voice of God)

Isaiah was also an audio prophet, which means he heard the audible voice of God and prophesied what he heard. God does still speak audibly to, not only the prophets, also to the entire Body of Christ. An audio prophet hears the voice of God and all of His inflections to speak His word in the earth. Audio prophets are also utilized to express the other audio forms of God's communication: laughter, singing, etc.

<u>International</u>

In 2016, many are teaching you can be an international ministry without traveling to other countries. This is not a God principle or a God rule, that is man-made. As we look at Isaiah, Isaiah is not noted for traveling but he is noted for speaking into and about other countries at the leading of the Lord. Prophets are not always traveling in the natural but they do travel in the Spirit. Many times prophets represent "the voice of the Lord walking", by prophesying the will of the Lord whether in a particular place or not.

Many prophets in the bible were impactful in other countries without going to those countries. If God is calling you to travel, get your passport and move. If God is calling you to prophesy from your living room, a church sanctuary, even a street corner - about another country, OBEY HIM! Do not get caught up in what man is saying is international ministry; just follow the instructions given to you by God.

<u>Isaiah Naked</u>

Prophets are used of God many times to illustrate prophecy. We see this with Hosea, Micah and Isaiah, just to name a few. In the 20th chapter of Isaiah, Isaiah is instructed to remove sackcloth and his sandals as a sign to Egypt and Ethiopia. Isaiah being naked and barefoot was a sign that Assyria was going to overtake Egypt and Ethiopia and the captives would be marched naked and barefoot through the streets. God will instruct prophets to become illustrations (rhema words) for the purpose of visual prophecy. We know about prophets having vision but did not realize they could prophesy visually. For three years, Isaiah complied and obeyed the instruction to be naked and barefoot.

<u>Christ Prophecies</u>

Almost one-third of the chapters of the book of Isaiah contain prophecies about Jesus Christ, addressing both His first and second comings. Isaiah provides more prophecy of the second coming of Christ than any other Old Testament prophet.

- He shall judge between the nations" (Isaiah 2:4).
- He was to be the "Branch of the Lord" (Isaiah 4:2; Isaiah 11:1).
- He would be born of a virgin and be called "Immanuel" (Isaiah 7:14; Isaiah 8:8,10).
- He would be a "stone of stumbling and a rock of offense" (Isaiah 8:14).
- An eternal "government will be upon His shoulder" and He would be called the "Prince of Peace" (Isaiah 9:6-7).
- The Holy Spirit would "rest upon Him" (Isaiah 11:2).
- He would be "a tried stone, a precious cornerstone, a sure foundation" (Isaiah 28:16).

The foretelling of Christ is a mainstream topic throughout the prophecy of Isaiah. The 53rd chapter of Isaiah is very profound in the unveiling of Christ's purpose. Isaiah is used to give such imagery of the life and death of Christ. The prophecies of Christ and the Kingdom of God are poetically woven throughout the book of Isaiah. The tapestry of Christ's revelation from birth to resurrection within the prophecy of Isaiah is a strategic manifestation of the Lord. Also, the kingdom of God is a main topic within the prophecies of Isaiah.

<u>Isaiah: Reminder of Identity</u>

Though a lot of the prophecy of Isaiah deals with the sin of nations, God also uses Isaiah to prophesy to the real identity of Israel. God uses prophets to speak beyond the flesh and sin to speak of what God has spoken and written of individuals and nations.

Many times Isaiah is used to remind Israel that they are God's servant and He chose them. Israel had to remember they did not choose God but He chose them from all the people of the earth (Isaiah 41:8-9; John 15:16). This is a lesson we need to learn in the 21st century, God chose us before we knew He was God.

Prophets are instrumental in establishing God's identity of men in the earth. Confusion comes to identity, the longer men are away from God through sin and rebellion. Prophets are used to realign men to their identity in and for God. The revealing of identity is God's seed of reconciliation and redemption.

Isaiah Prophesies Deliverance and Redemption
Isaiah was used to prophesy Israel's deliverance and redemption. God never leaves the earth without a remnant of His own that will stand as a sign of His power. Israel was not only His chosen people but His remnant (rescued, delivered) people.

God desires to deliver all people from sin for His own sake. He does not desire to see anyone in eternal damnation and wants all to come unto repentance (2 Peter 3:9). When God delivers us from sin, he does not remember our sin and He blots out our transgressions (Isaiah 43:25). In delivering Israel then, and us now, God is creating a remnant people who have been birthed of His spirit into the earth (Isaiah 46:3-4; John 3:1-8).

God paid a price to redeem us. That price was His son, Jesus Christ. He loved us so much, even when we were dying in sin, to send a redeemer of His spirit.

But when Christ appeared as a High Priest of the good things to come [that is, true spiritual worship], He entered through the greater and more perfect tabernacle, not made with hands, that is to say, not a part of this [material] creation. He went once for all into the Holy Place [the Holy of Holies of heaven, into the presence of God], and not through the blood of goats and calves, but through His own blood, having obtained and secured eternal redemption [that is, the salvation of all who personally believe in Him as Savior]. For if the sprinkling of [ceremonially] defiled persons with the blood of goats and bulls and the ashes of a [burnt] heifer is sufficient for the cleansing of the body, how much more will the blood of Christ, who through the eternal [Holy] Spirit willingly offered Himself unblemished [that is, without moral or spiritual imperfection as a sacrifice] to God, cleanse your conscience from dead works and lifeless observances to serve the ever living God? For this reason He is the Mediator and Negotiator of a new covenant [that is, an entirely new agreement uniting God and man], so that those who have been called [by God] may receive [the fulfillment of] the promised eternal inheritance, since a death has taken place [as the payment] which redeems them from the sins committed under the obsolete first covenant (Hebrews 9:11-15 AMP)

Isaiah's Death

Isaiah's death is another controversial one. Through many Hebraic accounts, Isaiah was sawn in half. Some say he was stretched between two horses and sawn in half. Some say he was hidden in a cedar tree and the tree and he were sawn in two. There is no scriptural backing for either opinion but Hebrews 11:37 makes mention of this type of death:

They were stoned, they were sawn asunder (in two), were tempted, were slain with the sword: they wandered about in sheepskins and goatskins; being destitute, afflicted, tormented; (Hebrews 11:37)

> Elijah is a prophet whose personal life is not revealed in scripture.

Chapter Four:

The Biography of Elijah

We do not see Elijah's family, all that is revealed is where he is from. Elijah is a Tishbite, meaning he is from Tishbe, which is in Gilead. Gilead is a mountainous area east of the Jordan River.

Prophetic Ministry

Elijah served as prophet during the reign of Ahab only. Ahab was an unrighteous king of Israel. He was king for twenty-two years and did more evil than any king before him (1 Kings 16:29-30).

Elijah's first prophetic word was against the dew. After this prophetic declaration, God instructed Elijah where and how He was going to provide for him (1 Kings 17:2-4). Elijah is an example of God's provision even when the land is going without. If there was no dew (rain) that meant there was to be a drought, which meant a very low to no harvest. God always provides for His remnant and obedient people, look at Elijah.

Elijah obeyed the instructions of the Lord. As He obeyed God, he was fed twice a day by ravens; bread and flesh, both day and night. Elijah drank from the brook. One day the brook dried up because there was no rain. Elijah had come to the end of the instruction and God is about to introduce a shift to Elijah's life (1 Kings 17:5-7).

Elijah is instructed to get to Zarepath and dwell there, and that a widow woman is going to sustain him. God speaks more to prophets about themselves than others. Elijah has received more instructions at this point about himself than Ahab. Prophets can be assigned to locales for particular assignments. Every instruction from God does not have the details immediately but the details will come as we continue to obey.

Elijah obeyed the voice of God in the shift. He gets to the gate of the city of Zarephath and meets the widow woman. He asks her for water. As she goes to get the water, he asks for a morsel (fragment, bit, piece) of bread. The widow woman gives Elijah a reason why she cannot do so. It is interesting that God sent Elijah to this woman to be taken care of and she is a part of the drought and preparing herself and her son to die. She is telling Elijah that she is struggling because she has so little that she cannot give him a cake of his own. God sends prophets to hard places to prove His miraculous power.

And Elijah said unto her, Fear not; go and do as thou hast said: but make me thereof a little cake first, and bring it unto me, and after make for thee and for thy son. For thus saith the Lord God of Israel, The barrel of meal shall not waste, neither shall the cruse of oil fail, until the day that the Lord sendeth rain upon the earth. And she went and did according to the saying of Elijah: and she, and he, and her house, did eat many days. And the barrel of meal wasted not, neither did the cruse of oil fail, according to the word of the Lord, which he spake by Elijah. (1 Kings 17:13-16)

Elijah's First Miracle

The widow woman's son got sick and there was no breath in him. He was dead. Elijah gets to the woman and she begins to ask some bizarre questions. She was wondering if Elijah was coming to recall her sin and slay her son. Elijah ignored her questions and requested the body of her son. Elijah takes the son to his loft, laid him on his bed and began to cry out to the Lord. Elijah then stretches himself across the boy three times and cried out to God for the son's soul to return to his body. After the prophet stretched out and cried out to the Lord, the Lord heard him and the son was revived and delivered to his mother. Elijah's first miracle is a resurrection. Prophets can be used to resurrect and revive those who have died or become dry in the things of God and life.

Confronting Ahab's Troubling of Israel

God instructs Elijah to shew himself to Ahab and then He would send the rain to the earth (1 Kings 18:1-2). One lesson prophets have to learn is to obey regardless if it makes sense to our flesh or not. The last instruction to Elijah does not seem to connect in any way. Why would showing himself to Ahab cause God to release rain? If Elijah spent too much time analyzing how it would work, he would disobey God. The rain was not immediate after Elijah showed himself to Ahab, either. We have to trust God, especially when there is no immediate manifestation, God cannot fail, we just need to faithfully obey.

God is about to bring order to Israel in Samaria and it starts with the leader. God never deals with the people before dealing with the leader. Ahab is said to have done more to provoke God to anger than any other king (1 Kings 16:33). Ahab challenges who Elijah is, questioning if he was troubling Israel. Elijah set him straight and told him:

And he answered, I have not troubled Israel; but thou, and thy father's house, in that ye have forsaken the commandments of the Lord, and thou hast followed Baalim. Now therefore send, and gather to me all Israel unto mount Carmel, and the prophets of Baal four hundred and fifty, and the prophets of the Groves four hundred, which eat at Jezebel's table. (Kings 18:18-19)

Prophets were sent to destroy systems that dishonor God. Elijah is about to destroy the false prophetic and idolatry that has run rampant under the leadership of Ahab. Ahab was told to gather the prophets of Baal and prophets of Grove (see Chapter Six). God does not deal with the people before dealing with their leadership. Ahab has been confronted and instructed, now Elijah turns to the people.

The people were challenged because they could not discern if they were serving God Almighty or Baal. Elijah confronts their confusions and instructs them to choose whom they will serve. As long as the people are between two opinions they cannot proper honor, worship or hear the voice of God. Elijah tells them you need to choose who is your God (Joshua 24:15).

After Elijah challenges the people, he instructs the prophets of Baal to prepare a sacrifice and call on their gods while he called the name of the Lord. He told them, the God that answers by fire, He would be God. The people agreed to the terms that Elijah put before all of Israel. The prophets of Baal prepared the offering and began calling on their gods. From the morning until noon, calling and calling and NOTHING! They are standing before the people calling on many gods and no one is answering.

The prophets of Baal leapt on the altar and began to act dramatically; trying to get their gods to answer them. Then

Elijah mocked them for all the theatrics of calling on their god.

After all the dramatics, to no avail of the prophets of Baal, Elijah begins to set order. He repairs the altar of the Lord, the place of sacrifice and worship that has been broken down. He gathered 12 stones, which represents each of the tribes of Israel. After which he made a trench that could hold two measures (about 80 liters) of seed. Elijah then put the wood in order, cut up the bullock, laid the bullock on the wood and asked for 4 barrels of water and poured it on the burnt offering. He instructed for 8 more barrels of water to be poured over the burnt offering. Now it is the time of the evening sacrifice and Elijah begins to pray:

And it came to pass at the time of the offering of the evening sacrifice, that Elijah the prophet came near, and said, Lord God of Abraham, Isaac, and of Israel, let it be known this day that thou art God in Israel, and that I am thy servant, and that I have done all these things at thy word. Hear me, O Lord, hear me, that this people may know that thou art the Lord God, and that thou hast turned their heart back again. (1 Kings 18:36-37)

God answers:
Then the fire of the Lord fell, and consumed the burnt sacrifice, and the wood, and the stones, and the dust, and licked up the water that was in the trench. And when all the people saw it, they fell on their faces: and they said, The Lord, he is the God; the Lord, he is the God.
(1 Kings 18:38-39)

After the fire of the Lord and the confession of the people, Elijah tells them to gather the prophets of Baal. They take the prophets of Baal to Kishon and slew them.

Kishon is a place of victory for the children of Israel, it is the same place of the defeat of Sisera under the leadership of prophetess and judge, Deborah.

<u>Retaliation against Elijah – Jezebel</u>

After the greatest victory of Elijah's prophetic ministry, Jezebel threatens to kill him. Elijah is now depressed and on the run, in fear for his life. Depression causes Elijah to pray for his own death. Prophets can fall into depression after a great conquest, especially if they are not properly covered and if they do not descend back into the earth (their person) gingerly. Depression is something that attempts to destroy prophets through their mind and emotions. Elijah has confronted prophets that focus on happiness and personal wealth, without godly accountability and the retaliation causes him to be in depression, wanting to die. Depression is a serious condition that, with Holy Spirit and even counseling, prophets will overcome and continue in the will of the Lord.

Depression will skew your perception, it did with Elijah. Elijah's perception was he was the only prophet, he was wrong. God had to correct and humble Elijah letting him know there were seven thousand prophets who had not bowed to Baal. Elijah's bout is an example to all prophets. Do not allow victories to become places of depression and suicidal thoughts. Depression caused Elijah to isolate himself and retreat to constant sleeping. The thing about Elijah's depression is he went to the mountain of God; even in a time of depression - get to where God is. Elijah retreats to a cave and soon God shows up and begins to ask him why he was there.

Elijah begins a continuous conversation with the Lord and even with an angel; yet, he still has a perception issue.

He is instructed to stand upon the mountain before the Lord. As he is standing before the Lord, there was a great wind, an earthquake and a fire and the Lord was not in any of them, many times we are looking for the Lord to be in the dramatics, when He is actually whispering because our lives are too busy, too loud and distracted. God uses the small still voice (His whisper) to draw us into a more intimate reality of His voice.

After hearing God's whispering to him and drawing him into a more intimate reality, Elijah wraps his face in his mantle (an expensive garment used to identify his ranking in society, probably a prayer shawl) and stands in the entrance of the cave he isolated himself in. God begins to speak in His normal voice and asks Elijah a question: *What are you doing here?* The small still voice will still your spirit, so you can hear where God really wants to speak to you. Elijah begins to tell God all he has done but the reality is he feels alone and that he is marked for death. The small still voice will still you so you can address yourself in the Lord.

After Elijah pours out his emotions, the Lord begins to instruct him about his next assignment. Many times the Lord hears our emotions, but will speak to our destiny and purpose before addressing our emotions. Elijah was told to anoint the next king of Syria, the next king of Israel and the prophet who would occupy his place in the earth (an inherited son). These kings and prophet would become a government network of checks and balances that could not destroy what God was establishing in the land.

Word Against Ahab and Jezebel
Elijah was given a very stern word for both Ahab and Jezebel. Ahab was going to take possession of Naboth's vineyard after he was stoned, Elijah was told to meet him.

The word of the Lord begins, that as dogs are licking the blood of Naboth, so would they lick the blood of Ahab. Elijah then tells Ahab that he sold himself to work evil in the sight of the Lord. The Lord says He will cut off the posterity and the males (those that piss on the wall) of Ahab. This word is very direct, the Lord, is cutting off all that would reproduce through Ahab's lineage. The word continues that Ahab would be like Jeroboam and Baasha who provoked Him and caused Israel to sin. God says that dogs will eat the males of Ahab that die in the city and if they die in the field, fowls (vultures) of the air will eat them. God repeats that there is none like Ahab who followed the idols of Amorites that God removed from the children of Israel. Ahab heard this word and humbled himself by renting his clothes, putting on sackcloth and fasting. The Lord then told Elijah, all that was spoken would not happen to Elijah but would manifest in the time of his son. The word is fulfilled in 2 Kings 10:1-11.

The word to Jezebel starts that she will be eaten by dogs. This prophetic word was fulfilled by the hands of Jehu in 2 Kings 9:30-37.

Calling Fire From Heaven

Moab rebelled against Israel after the death of Ahab. Ahaziah, king of Samaria, fell off a lattice and became sick. He sent messengers to enquire of Beelzebub, the god of Akron. An angel of the Lord tells Elijah to meet the messengers and challenge them for not seeking the God of Israel. After challenging the messengers, Elijah prophesies the king will not recover. The messengers return to Ahaziah and tell him what was said to them. The king perceived that the man who spoke these things, was Elijah.

Ahaziah sends captains with fifty soldiers to Elijah. There were two teams of fifty-one sent to Elijah who were consumed by the fire Elijah called down from heaven. The third team was not consumed but Elijah went down with the captain as the angel of the Lord instructed him. Elijah gets to the king and repeats what has already been spoken and the king dies as the word said.

Elijah's Ascension

Elijah and Elisha travel to Bethel and Jericho. Elijah tells Elisha to stay in those places, but Elisha refused and continued to follow Elijah. In both cities, the sons (company) of prophets asked Elisha about Elijah ascension. Elisha responds each time that he knows God's plan and told them to hold their peace.

Now they are at Jordan. Elijah folded his mantle and struck the water and the waters part. Once on the other side, Elisha asks for a double portion of Elijah's spirit to be upon him. Elijah tells him this is a hard thing but if you see me when I go up, it will be unto you. They continued to talk and walk, then a chariot of fire with horses of fire appears. Elijah is taken up in a whirlwind into heaven. Elijah, like Enoch, never saw physical death. Elijah's ascension is a prophetic sign that death is not required of all men.

Elijah is mentioned in the Gospels and in the book of James. The mount Transfiguration account of Jesus talking with Moses and Elijah is one of the main mentions. When James mentions Elijah as an example of having passions like we all do, but he still earnestly prayed and the rain stopped, he prayed again and the rain fell and earth brought forth fruit.

We must look at these overlooked prophets to understand seasons in our personal prophetic lives and ministries.

Chapter Five:

The Biography of Overlooked Prophets

As the biographer of prophets, for the purpose of this book, I see some who have been overlooked. We read the scriptures that bear their name but we do not understand their significance to the legacy of prophetic lineage, heritage and inheritance. We must look at these overlooked prophets to understand seasons in our personal prophetic lives and ministries.

Anna, The Temple Prophet

Anna, is overlooked many times, because she does not have an extensive mention in scripture. The truth is, her story is only three verses in Luke's account of the Gospel. Though a very short story it is powerful and it is noteworthy.

Anna is the daughter of Phanuel who is of the tribe of Aser (or Asher). Asher is the eighth son of Jacob. Not much more is known of Anna's lineage. She was married, so she was a woman of covenant. When she got married she was a virgin and was married to her husband for seven years before she became widowed. Sexual morality is important to the prophetic call. One of the tactics of hell against prophets is to seduce (draw them away) them into sexual immorality and idolatry. Anna was pure unto her marriage; she did not offer herself to perversion of sexualities.

Anna was of great age. She had been widowed for 84 years. In the midst of those 84 years, she decided not to leave the temple. She purposed to give her live as a sacrifice unto the Lord. In that sacrifice, she dedicated her life to prayer and fasting, both night and day. Prophets must remain prayerful and consecrated through prayer and fasting. Through Anna's life of prayer and fasting, it kept her thankful. It is important for prophets (all believers for that matter) to be thankful in all things. When prophets are not thankful they become pessimistic and focus on dark things, not the light of God.

Anna spoke to all who were looking for redemption from the Lord. Her prophetic focus became redemption as she prayed, fasted and gave thanks. There are no records of prophecies through Anna but her prophetic ministry is a powerful example of prophetic seasons and timings. She is an example of staying in the presence of God, consecrating and allowing His redemptive power to be expressed through her life. Prophets must remember we are used in seasons and cycles and every season and cycle is not the same. Be content with how God has chosen to use you and obey Him at all costs.

Silas, The Team Prophet

Silas was a team prophet. God used him to work with other prophets and apostles to fulfill the will of God. Silas is another prophet who does not have recorded prophetic words but his ministry is important to understanding prophets and prophetics. The apostles and elders chose

Silas to go with Paul and Barnabas and other prophets to Antioch, Syria and Cilicia. Silas, being a team prophet is seeing exhorting the people of God with Judas (not Iscariot).

After an issue between Paul and Barnabas over John Mark, Paul chose Silas to travel with him to Syria and Cilicia to strengthen and confirm the churches there. Silas began to travel extensively with Paul and they became the foreshadow of the apostolic prophetic team. Churches were established in faith and increased in number as Paul and Silas carried the word of the Lord and obeyed God together.

Paul and Silas went to Macedonia after Paul had a vision. As they traveled, they came to the chief city of Macedonia, which is Philippi. On the Sabbath, they came to the city near the river to a prayer gathering. They sat down and began to speak to the women there. They encountered a woman named Lydia. She is a businesswoman. Paul began to speak the things of the Lord and Lydia's heart was opened to the truth of God. She was baptized, then her household and she began to take care of Paul and Silas.

They went to another prayer meeting and encountered a girl possessed with divination. This girl was not only a slave to this demonic oppression but also to men who used her for financial gain. She began to follow the apostolic team and loudly proclaim (in mocking fashion), "These men are the servants of the Most High God, which shew us the way of salvation." She followed them for days loudly speaking this statement over and over again. Paul became grieved and cast the spirit out of the girl, setting her free; which caused Paul and Silas to be beaten and imprisoned for the cause of Christ.

Prophets, be aware that demons like to come to prayer meetings to cause disruptions and distractions. Divination, witchcraft and spirits like them, do not want people of God to know the power of prayer. As vessels of constant prayer, the lives of prophets should be continuous testimonies of what prayer can do and how in prayer we overcome the attempts, tactics and attacks of hell.

Paul and Silas are in prison, the inner prison (dungeon), and it becomes midnight. There is something about prophets and midnight. They begin to pray and sing praises unto God. These men are bound, have been beaten and lied on, but still find strength to pray and praise God. Prophets are examples of going through and coming through all things with prayer and praise! Everybody heard Paul and Silas, they were not ashamed of the God they called upon. This impromptu praise service caused a natural response, an earthquake. The apostle and prophet doing spiritual things caused a natural reaction that was a breakthrough for all in earshot. The one charged to watch Paul and Silas begins to panic and become suicidal but Paul instructs him not to harm himself and he asks, "What must I do to be saved?" The jailer hears the word of God, washed Paul and Silas' wounds, was baptized and his household. He then fed the apostle and prophet and they all rejoiced. Even in your times of challenge, if you continue doing what is right others will receive God.

Too often prophets are seen as lone rangers. But as we look at Silas' ministry throughout the book of Acts, he is always teamed with at least one other prophet. Prophets have to learn to work in team fashion. No prophet has it all, we all see, hear and prophesy in part, so we need each other to fulfill our call. Silas was teamed with Judas, teamed with Paul and teamed with Timotheus, no one fought for position, and everyone did their particular part of the assignment. Prophets, embrace team ministry.

Silas' ministry disproves all attempts to teach that prophets work alone in ministry. Sadly, we have yet again received some errant teaching. Eagles represent prophets and the prophetic; many of us were taught and received that eagles soar alone, but this is not true of all eagles. Most eagles actually soar and fly together; it is called convocation when eagles gather. So, prophets have to learn to gather and team up for the purposes of God.

Deborah, The Mother in Israel

When Deborah emerges, it is in the midst of oppression. We must be aware that many prophets are birthed and mantled during the oppression of those they are called and assigned to. Deborah was probably a prophetess before the oppression started, but the recognition of her prophethood and judgeship started amidst the oppression. Deborah is one of few women named prophetess in the bible. Today, there is a great debate on whether women should be called prophets or prophetesses; this debate is raging but not beneficial. Whether women are called prophets or prophetesses, they need to be obedient to God and fulfill their assignment.

Deborah was a wife, a woman of covenant. Her husband's name is Lapidoth. Not much is mentioned about her husband. Deborah was a judge. Judges ruled Israel before they ever had a king. She served as one that made judgment between the children of Israel. She made judges between Ramah and Bethel in Mount Ephraim. Deborah was a prophetess who ruled over government, she led the nation.

With her ability to rule and judge, as well as being a

prophetess, she became a military strategist. She spoke to Barak, the general of the army, speaking the word of the Lord. With the word of the Lord in his ear, Barak told Deborah, "I will obey, but only if you go with me". Barak made Deborah his co-general. She became the vessel of military strategy through prophetic wisdom and revelation. Through Deborah's strategic prophetic releases, Barak and the army won over the enemies that were causing warfare and oppression to the children of Israel.

The entire fifth Chapter of Judges is a song of deliverance, a duet with Deborah and Barak. They are a testament of team ministry: breaking barriers, blazing trails and accomplishing the goal. After the deliverance of the children of Israel - after the oppression - there were forty years of rest upon the land.

Deborah was a woman who was recognized. Many say during old testament times, women had no value. Deborah debunks that. She was a prophetess, a judge and a military strategist. She was a woman, yes, but she was also a leader who was honored for her ability to fulfill her assignment. She walked with Barak, not behind him, not under him; although he was the general of the army. Deborah is a multifaceted prophetess and she should be seen as a standard for women to not be oppressed by traditions of men. Deborah is a trailblazer, she was the first. She does not have to be the last.

Deborah is a mother in Israel. She carried Israel from the point of oppression to 40 years of peace. Deborah was impregnated with the victory that Israel needed through her function as a prophetess, judge and military strategist. As you look even closer at the life and ministry of Deborah; you will see she worked with the princes (leaders) of Issachar. Issachar is a strategic tribe knowing the times and seasons and what must be done (1 Chronicles 12:32). Deborah was a woman of rank who was sharpened by those she labored and associated with.

Her ministry shows that prophets can be called to multifaceted ministry and fulfill each part well. Never let all the multiplicities of your assignment cause you to lose excellence for the kingdom of God. Do all things well and unto God.

Agabus, The Warning Prophet

Agabus may be a name you are not familiar with. He is mentioned among the prophets who came to the Antioch church after Saul (later Paul) and Barnabas remained there a year and taught the people of God. Agabus traveled with a company (team) of prophets from Jerusalem to the Antioch church. Once at Antioch, Agabus prophesies about a dearth (scarcity of harvest; famine) in the land. This prophetic word was fulfilled during the reign of the fourth Roman emperor, Claudius Caesar.

Agabus later prophesies to Paul, using his own girdle, about being bound by Jews and delivered unto the Gentiles. He was an illustrative prophet as he used Paul's girdle to bind his own hands and feet. After hearing the word of the Lord, they begged Paul not to go to Jerusalem and he spoke boldly that he was ready to be bound and even die for the name of Jesus Christ.

Agabus was a prophet used to warn of future events. His ministry was used to prepare people for what was going to happen next. He was not prophesying in regards to discipline or judgment, but the course of events as God saw them. Agabus gives us a glimpse of how prophets are used to warn in the New Testament, just like in the Old Testament. He is also a sign of prophets working and traveling together for the work of the Lord.

Miriam, The Praising Prophet

Moses has just led the children of Israel out of bondage. They are fleeing Pharaoh and his army and come to the Red Sea. God causes the Red Sea to stand up like walls that the children of Israel would crossover on dry land. When the last Israelite that crossed over, the walls came down and drowned Pharaoh and his army. Miriam gets a tambourine and so do the other women and they begin to play and dance. The women led praise for the victory they just received by the miraculous power of God. Miriam functioned as a minstrel. A minstrel is a prophet who is also a musician. As she took that tambourine and began to praise she was no longer just a prophet who could speak or write, now she was a prophet of sound.

Miriam became a leper because she and Aaron allowed their flesh to speak unrighteous things. They did not like Moses' choice of a wife because she was an Ethiopian. This is a heart issue, expressing a racial issue. They did not have an issue with how she acted or treated their brother, only her race. Prophets have to be delivered from their natural idiosyncrasies. If natural idiosyncrasies are not healed and delivered they will become a weak place within that will hinder ministry.

Aaron and Miriam then allowed envy and jealousy to speak through them. They began to ask "Is Moses the only one God is speaking to, doesn't He speak to us too?" This is a dangerous place for prophets as well. The place of comparison is a slap in God's face, as if He does not know who to use. As they are talking to each other the Lord hears them. He calls Aaron, Moses and Miriam out of the tabernacle. God begins to deal with Aaron and Miriam on how He establishes a prophet in the land. He explains that

Moses is not an ordinary prophet because he speaks with him mouth to mouth, not in dark (hidden) speech and in similitude of the Lord. He questions how they could speak against His servant and His anger was kindled against them. The cloud departed and Miriam became a leper.

Miriam's punishment for speaking against Moses, the Lord's servant, was instant. We need to realize we do not know when God will execute His judgment against us. Aaron realized the wrong of his and Miriam's actions and told Moses that they were foolish and had sinned. He asked that Moses not allow Miriam to die. Moses begins to pray. One thing prophets will have to learn to do is pray and not respond in the flesh. Aaron and Miriam were rejecting and dishonoring Moses on multiple levels. Moses is not dealing with them in his flesh but in the Spirit. Moses asked the Lord to heal her. God responds she will be separated for seven days then He will receive her again.

Miriam represents prophets with an authentic call but need deliverance from carnal thinking and speaking. Though she was used to lead praise after a great deliverance, she needed personal deliverance. She experienced discipline for allowing her flesh to speak against God's servant and her leader. Miriam was a leader of the children of Israel like Moses but she was not the senior leader. Allowing herself to speak and compare herself to Moses got her in trouble. She is healed because of the prayers of the very one she spoke against. After her healing, we do not see Miriam functioning in ministry anymore in scripture. Miriam died and was buried in Kadesh.

Iddo, The Grandfather Prophet

Iddo may not be a name you are familiar with. Iddo is a multifaceted prophet recognized in the Old Testament. He is only mentioned in ten verses of scripture but he is worth looking at.

Iddo is referenced as both a prophet and a seer. He is known for his ability to see and hear in the realm of the Spirit. Most are referenced as one or the other, but Iddo is both. He is a rarity as he flows equally in both streams of prophetic manifestation.

Iddo lived during the reigns of Solomon, Rehoboam and Abijah. Rehobam succeeds his father as king and during his reign, ten tribes crowned Jeroboam as their king. The only tribes that remained with Rehoboam were Judah and Benjamin (1 Kings 12:1-21).

Iddo is a writer. He is identified as writing the visions against Jeroboam. Some of the greatest prophetic revelation and release is written. We have focused on the verbal prophecy and have missed those who have an anointing to transcribe the word of God. Iddo is credited with three texts within scripture: the visions of Iddo the seer against Jeroboam; the book of Iddo concerning genealogies and the story of the prophet Iddo. These texts include acts of King Solomon, visions against Jeroboam, the acts of Rehoboam and the acts of Abijah. The writing of God's prophet covers three kings ruling the people of God. Iddo represents the scribal prophets that God utilizes in many seasons to establish His word. We are accustomed to prophets declaring (speaking out), but it is not as common as prophets that decree (write) the word of God.

Iddo is the root of a prophetic lineage. He is the grandfather to prophet Zechariah. We have become common with spiritual lineages of prophets but not natural. Here we see Iddo, a prophet and seer, has a lineage and heritage beyond himself. Scripture does not express if

Zechariah's father, Berechiah, is a prophet or not. Berechiah's natural and spiritual profession is not mentioned, but to have a father and son as prophets, must have been interesting to say the least.

Iddo represents prophets that do not do much prophetic ministry in the pulpit, but they can write the word of God just the same. These prophets are as much prophets as those who are constantly speaking the word of God. One of the worst things we, as the ecclesia, can do is reject a prophet for not ministering the way we perceive they should.

Huldah, The Sought Out Prophet

Josiah, The Boy King

Josiah, an eight-year-old, has just become king of Judah. This is unprecedented for a child to become king at such a young age. King Josiah was not like his forefathers, Manasseh and Amon, who ruled unrighteous in the eyesight of God (1 Kings 21). Josiah is known for following after the order of King David, God's righteous king.

In the eighteenth year of Josiah's reign, the book of the law was found. The king heard the book of the law as his scribe, Shaphan, read it. After hearing the book of the law, Josiah sent five men to Huldah, the prophetess, for understanding. Josiah was concerned about the wrath of God upon the people of Judah because their fathers had not hearkened (heard and obeyed) to the words of the book of the law.

Huldah, a woman of covenant, is married to Shallum. Shallum is the keeper of the king's wardrobe. Huldah lived in Jerusalem in a college. A college is known as "the second order" or "second rank". Five men began to commune with Huldah about the book of the law. Huldah begins to prophesy that all that the king had read was going to happen. The people had forsaken Him and began to burn incense unto other gods, the people were found in false worship. The Lord has been provoked to anger and His wrath is kindled and He proclaims it will not be quenched. The prophecy continues directly for King Josiah that because he was tender towards the Lord, rent his clothes and wept that the Lord would not allow him to see the word come to pass, he would die before it happened.

Huldah is a contemporary of Jeremiah and Zephaniah; all three were in active ministry during the reign of King Josiah. Huldah is an expository prophet. She was used to gain understanding from what had already been written as the book of the law. Prophets need to remember that God will use them to bring clarity and understanding to what was produced before their birth. Prophets are used to expose and teach the word of God and are to be those who study in depth the word of God. These prophets are not dependent upon spontaneous revelation only, but the written word of God as well.

Jehu, The Governmental Leader Confronting Prophet

Most times when we hear the name Jehu we think of the king anointed by Elijah to overtake Jezebel. That Jehu is the son of Nimishi. However, there is Jehu, son of Hanani, who is a prophet. The prophetic word through Jehu was to a wicked king of Israel, Baasha. Hanani is a seer who rebuked King Asa and then was imprisoned (2 Chronicles 16:7-10). Jehu has a prophetic lineage of governmental confrontation for the Lord.

Jehu is a prophet who does not prophesy often but is still important to the purposes of God. Jehu was not prophesying to religious leaders or to the people but directly to a governmental leader. God choose Baasha to rule Israel after Jeroboam, who was wicked, and Baasha followed in the wicked leadership causing Israel to sin. Jeroboam was the first king of Israel after the split of the kingdom after Solomon's death. Jeroboam ushered a season of idolatry and idol worship in Israel. Jehu is raised up to prophesy to king Baasha because of his wicked leadership. The prophecy pertains to taking the posterity (lineage, heritage) and making it like the house of Jeroboam (1Kings 14:1-19).

Jehu's prophetic utterance was released futuristically. It did not come to pass in the season he prophesied it, but was fulfilled during the reign of Elah, Baasha's son and successor. The traitor, Zimiri, who killed Elah, fulfilled the prophetic word and all the posterity of Baasha said (1 Kings 16:1-12).

Jehu is also recorded as confronting Jehoshaphat, king of Judah. Jehu was used in both the northern and southern parts of the kingdom, Israel and Judah. He was used to rebuke Jehoshaphat who was in alliance with Ahab. Jehoshaphat and Ahab went into battle together at Ramoth-Gilead where Ahab died. Jehu challenged Jehoshaphat's willingness to partner with the ungodly and to love those who hate the Lord. These are the same things that need to be confronted in the 21st century. We cannot align with that which is against God's standard and believe that God is all right with it. We cannot be friends with enemies of our Lord. Though Jehoshaphat had an alliance with Ahab, God still found good things within him. During his reign he took away the Groves (Asherah poles/trees for idol/goddess worship on the altars) and prepared his heart to seek the Lord. After being rebuked and affirmed by Jehu, Jehoshaphat returns the people from Beersheba to Mount

Ephraim to true worship unto the Lord God (2 Chronicles 19:1-4).

<u>Shemaiah, The Strategic Prophet</u>

Shemaiah is a prophet who was raised during a time of intended war between kings Jeroboam and Rehoboam. The king of Judah, Rehoboam, was ready to wage war against Jerusalem's King Jeroboam. Shemaiah was used to instruct Rehoboam and Judah (the tribes of Judah and Benjamin) not to war with Israel and return to their homes. They obeyed the word of the Lord.

Rehoboam got prideful after establishing the kingdom and strengthening himself and decided to forsake the law of God. This rebellion opened the door for the king of Egypt, Shishak, to come against the people of God. Rebellion causes the defenses of God to be removed from our lives and opens us to the enemy. Shishak came against twelve hundred chariots, sixty thousand horsemen and a people without number and took all the fenced (walled) cities pertaining to Judah. Pride and rebellion will cause enemies to overcome us if we do not repent.

Rehoboam and the princes of Judah were gathered in Jerusalem and Shemaiah is raised again to prophesy. The word that is released deals with the forsaken of the Lord and how the Lord left them to the hands of Shishak, the king of Egypt. Shishak overtakes Jerusalem and takes the treasures of the house of the Lord; the treasure is in the king's house and the shields of gold made by Solomon. Everything that had value was now in the hands of the king of Egypt because of pride and rebellion, which caused a forsaking of the Lord. There is a point were Rehoboam humbles himself and the Lord turned His wrath from him, not to destroy him totally and matters in Judah began to go well. All the acts of Rehobam and his seventeen-year tenure as king are recorded in the book of Shemaiah the prophet, 2 Chronicles 12.

Shemaiah is another prophet used to prophesy directly to governmental leaders. The prophecies that came from Shemaiah were of instruction and understanding, they reveal victory and failures in the decisions of Rehoboam and Judah. As a writer, Shemaiah wrote the acts of the king of Judah. It seems that prophets writing is important to the king, those of you that have vision to write, write. We need the scribal anointing of prophets in the 21st century.

Azariah and Oded, The Prophetic Team

Oded and Azariah are a father-son prophetic team. As we see them emerge in scripture, Azariah prophesies first. They were prophets during the reign of King Asa. Asa was the king of Judah and did what was right in the eyesight of the Lord (1 Kings 15). Asa's heart was perfect in all his ways before the Lord. Through the tag team ministry of Azariah and Oded, Asa took courage and put away, removed, took down all abominable idols from Judah, Benjamin and all the cities that had been conquered from mount Ephraim. Asa then renewed the altar of God, he restored the place of sacrifice and worship unto the Lord. Prophets are used to confront structures of false worship and idolatrous altars. After the prophetic word, Asa begins to purge all that he was king over.

After the restoring of the altar of the Lord, Asa gathers Judah and Benjamin along with strangers from Ephraim, Manasseh and Simeon, and fell prostrate as it was made known that the Lord God was with Asa. In the fifteenth year of his reign the people offered to the Lord the spoil that had attained. The spoil was seven hundred oxen and seven thousand sheep; they sacrificed and offered this spoil to the Lord as a covenant. The covenant was to seek the Lord of their fathers with all their heart and soul and whoever did not seek the Lord God of Israel was to be put to death. What a covenant Judah made after being purged of idols. Now all they wanted to be associated with, was the Lord God of Israel! Asa was so serious about his covenant and oath with God that he removed his mother from being queen because she built an idol. He cut it down, stamped it and burned it at the brook Kidron. How many of us have that dimension of loyalty to God, even when it comes to family? If you will not honor my God, you cannot be around me. The covenant caused peace in the land, for thirty-five years there was no war in the land of Judah.

During the reign of King Azah, king of Judah, Oded was used to prophesy again. Azah reigned for sixteen years and did not do what was righteous before the Lord. Azah was ushering polytheism into Judah, as Baalim is the plural of Baal. He began to make molten images unto Baalim for the purpose of worship. With the introduction of multiple gods, the worship instituted by Azah included sacrificing children by fire, burning incense in high places, on hills and even under trees. After accepting this false worship style, and forsaking the Lord, Judah was delivered into the hands of Syria, which took them captive and brought them to Damascus. Once in Damascus, Judah was delivered into the hand of Israel. Pekak, the captain of the army, slew one hundred and twenty thousand of Judah's valiant men because they forsook the Lord of their fathers. Again, when we turn away from God, we become open to the victory of our enemies over us. Azah, as the king, led the people away from God and now they were being captured and killed because of that turning away.

They had captured two hundred thousand people of

Judah and a great spoil is coming to Samaria. Oded meets the returning army of Israel. Oded begins to tell them the Lord delivered Judah into their hands, but they killed them with a rage that reached unto the heavens. He continues and questions them about making Judah slaves, while they are guilty of transgressing against the Lord as well. Oded instructs them to release the two hundred thousand they have just captured because the burning anger of God is against them. After Oded prophesies, four of the leaders took a stand against the return soldiers and told them you cannot do this, we are already guilty before God and this will add to our sins. The prophesying of Oded led to the deliverance of two hundred thousand people of Judah as the soldiers released them and the spoil they had attained.

Oded is used to give perception deliverance to Israel. As he prophesies he shows that Israel is not in any better place than Judah. Both Judah and Israel had transgressed against God, so Israel could not celebrate their victory because sin never wins over sin. Oded is the type of prophet that when he prophesies, it causes leaders to set order and repent of their perception and their thoughts of grandeur.

<u>John the Baptist, The Forerunner Prophet</u>

Why is John the Baptist amongst the overlooked prophets? Most times when we hear about John the Baptist, it is not mentioned that he is a prophet. We know he is the forerunner of Christ but we have not been taught about his prophethood.

John the Baptist is the son of Zacharias and Elisabeth. Elisabeth was barren and now her and her husband are old. Barrenness is nothing to God; He is about to show His supernatural ability to birth. Remember, Isaac? Zacharias was from a priestly lineage as he is of the course of Abia

(Abijah). As he was fulfilling his assignment as the priest, an angel came and began to speak with him. The angel began to release a prophetic utterance about Elisabeth bearing a son and his name being John. The angel continues and says that John will not drink wine and he will be filled with the Holy Ghost. The angel also prophetically reveals that John will come in the spirit of Elijah (Elias).

Sadly, Zacharias challenged the prophecy of the angel because of his and his wife's old age. After challenging the word, the angel revealed that he will be dumb and unable to speak until the manifestation of the word is accomplished. When John was delivered, his naming was controversial because John was not a name in his family. Zacharias asked for a writing table and wrote that his son's name was John and his tongue was loosed and he began to speak and praise God. Yet again, another miraculously born prophet.

Isaiah and Malachi prophesied of John the Baptist's assignment in the earth (Isaiah 40:3; Malachi 4:5-6). Hundreds of years before his birth God saw to prophesy about what he would do. John the Baptist is the cousin of Jesus Christ as well as His forerunner. He went forth before Jesus to set the stage for all Jesus would do. John the Baptist started his ministry in the wilderness of Judea and eventually ventured out to Jerusalem and to the Jordan. He is known as the Baptist (not the denomination) because he baptized people as they confessed their sins. One of his strongest messages is, "bring forth the fruit of repentance". Many of us have not been taught repentance properly, we think that all we have to do is say "Lord, I am sorry" to repent. We have to decide to turn away from the sin and submit to the order of God to actually repent.

He instructs the people that their (our) repentance must produce a tangible, visible change unto the Lord. He teaches that he baptizes with water unto repentance, but that the one coming after him will be baptizing with fire. Jesus soon comes to be baptized of him. After the baptism, the heavens opened, the Spirit of God came down like a dove, lighting upon him. All who were present heard a voice from heaven say, *"This is My beloved Son, in whom I am well pleased"*.

Jesus begins to affirm John the Baptist. He says, of those born of a woman there has not been one greater than him. This is a powerful statement. Jesus said that of John the Baptist, yet many of us overlook him. We do not see the significance of his life or ministry, but Jesus did.

Jesus asked his disciples about man's thoughts of him. Since many people did not know how to receive Jesus they thought he was everyone including John the Baptist. The disciples later begin to ask why the scribes expected Elijah to come first. And Jesus teaches them Elijah will come first and restore all things and he has already come. Jesus continues, they did not know he had come and the disciples understood it was John the Baptist. John the Baptist is the second prophet to carry the spirit of Elijah. Elisha was the first.

Herod killed John the Baptist for telling him the truth. Herod married his brother's wife and John told him that was unlawful. Herod jailed him for his new wife's sake, for if she had the authority she would have killed him. Herod feared her because John the Baptist was a just and holy man. On his birthday, he told his stepdaughter she could have anything up to half of his kingdom. She went to her mother and her mother said, "the head of John the Baptist". Herod kept his oath to his stepdaughter and had John the Baptist beheaded. John the Baptist was literally jailed and killed for expressing the law of God.

John the Baptist is another bold prophet confronting ungodly systems to restore order. Scripture expresses that from the time of John the Baptist, the kingdom of God experienced violence. There was a period of about four hundred years where there was no record of God speaking. John the Baptist emerges as the first prophet after God's silence and he is prophesying about repentance and the one to come after him. People did not know how to handle him, thought he was crazy and had a devil in him, because of his eating patterns. He stood out, his life and ministry were not status quo or boxed in by the traditions of men.

<u>Nathan, The King's Prophet</u>

Nathan served during the reigns of Kings David and Solomon. Nathan emerges as David has received rest from his enemies and now desires to make God a house. He was not comfortable with living in a cedar house and the ark of God being behind curtains. Nathan encourages him to do what is in his heart as the Lord is with him. God uses Nathan to explain to David about walking with Israel being in tents and the tabernacle but never asking for a house of cedar to be built. Then God uses Nathan to tell David about his destiny. He reminds him that he was taken from the sheepfold and pasture to be ruler over Israel and of the deliverance from all his enemies. God declares that he is going to establish David's house and even after his death, He will raise Solomon to build His house.

Nathan uses a parable to rebuke David. He tells a story of two men: one rich and one poor. The rich man had an abundance of everything. The poor man had one lamb that was like a part of his family. The rich man, being selfish, stole the poor man's lamb to feed a visitor that came to the city. David got upset at the parable and felt the man needed to make restitution because of his lack of compassion.

Nathan boldly proclaimed, "You are the Man". God begins to remind David of all He had done for him. God questions David's willingness to despise His word and do evil in His sight. David is then rebuked for taking Uriah's wife and making her his wife. Though David did this in secret, God was going to punish him in the light before all of Israel. David realized he has sinned and tells it to Nathan. Nathan then tells David though you will not die, your son that will be born will die. The son dies, but David and Bathsheba (the wife he was rebuked about) had another son. David named him Solomon and the Lord loved him, loved him so much he named Solomon, Jedidah. Jedidah literally means "Beloved of the Lord".

Nathan is used to anoint Solomon as king. David has gotten sick and is old. Adonjah claims the throne and began to reign. He gathered a counsel to help him take the throne. He slew many animals preparing for a royal celebration. While this is happening, Nathan has a meeting with Bathsheba. He counsels her on how to handle the situation and how he would help her. After Bathsheba and Nathan talk to David, David instructs Nathan and Zadok, the priest, to go to Gihon and anoint Solomon king and to sound the trumpet. Adonjah feared Solomon and thought he would take his life so he ran and took the horns of the altar. Solomon hears about him having the horns of the altar and says if he is found worthy none of his hair will hit the ground, but if he be found wicked, he will die. When Adonjah showed himself to Solomon he was sent to his house.

Nathan is another prophet-writer. He has a book that carries his name with all the acts of both kings David and Solomon, first to last. This is a testament that his prophet ministry lasted for the entirety of both reigns.

Prophets will always be needed as long as there is an earth. Man can overlook and ignore them, but God still sees them as important. God speaks to all types of men and women as His prophets. One lesson all prophets have to learn and embrace, if the people reject the word, they are actually rejecting God and not you. People are responsible for what they have heard through God's prophets whether they obey or forbear.

False prophets are impostors, attempting to look like God's prophets.

Chapter Six:

The False Prophets

False prophets speak lies, work divination, function by Baal (demonic network), reveal false visions and speak from the deceit of their heart to lead men and women astray. They also function using seduction, leading to fornication and idol worship. Nothing that comes from a false prophet is pure, aligns with scripture or properly positions those that hear what they say. They teach falsehoods and they are impure in all their functions. False prophets are impostors attempting to look like God's prophets. They are not sent from heaven's dispatch, they are sent from hell's dispatch.

Jesus teaches and warns against false prophets. He tells us to beware of them because they appear to be like you, but inwardly their motive is your destruction (Matthew 7:15). He also teaches and warns that they will come with great signs and wonders and if it were possible the elect would be deceived (Matthew 24:11-14). A true sign or miracle will cause worship unto God, but the signs and wonders of false prophets are to seduce (draw away from the right path). We have to be discerning of what is being presented to us. The enemy is very cunning and wants to deceive the people of God, to draw them away from God.

As true prophets are to draw us to God, false prophets are to draw us to satan.

John, the apostle, picks up the warning in his first epistle. He warns not to believe every spirit and to try the spirits to see if they are of God. The apostle instructs that any spirit from God would confess that Jesus Christ came in the flesh and any spirit that did not confess that, was of the antichrist. False prophets are fueled by the antichrist because prophecy is the testimony of Jesus Christ, any spirit or "prophet" who cannot testify of Jesus is false.

For they prophesy a lie unto you, to remove you far from your land; and that I should drive you out, and ye should perish. (Jeremiah 27:10)

The priests said not, Where is the LORD? and they that handle the law knew me not: the pastors also transgressed against me, and the prophets prophesied by Baal, and walked after things that do not profit. (Jeremiah 2:8)

Then the LORD said unto me, The prophets prophesy lies in my name: I sent them not, neither have I commanded them, neither spake unto them: they prophesy unto you a false vision and divination, and a thing of nought, and the deceit of their heart. (Jeremiah 14:14)

The False Prophets

Noadiah

This false prophetess was confronted during the time of Nehemiah and the rebuilding of the wall. She, along with other false prophets and Sanballat and Tobiah, tried to discourage, sabotage and stop the work of the Lord.

This type of false prophet attempts to intimidate and cause fear where God has blessed and the people are unified. Noadiah prophesies falsely of destruction and failure when there is already manifested success. She was paid by Sanballat and Tobiah to cause contention amongst the workers with Nehemiah. Noadiah is likened to Balak who tried to pay for a curse to be spoken over Israel.

Prophets of Baal and Prophets of Grove

During the time of Elijah, he had a showdown with some false prophets. These false prophets came in two categories: prophets of Baal and prophets of Grove.

Baal was the supreme deity of the Canaanites. Baal became an issue for Israel on many occasions. When they forsook the Lord and His commandments, many times they worshipped Baal. During the showdown, Baal was proven to be non-existent as his prophets were cutting themselves, jumping on the altar and other theatrics to get his attention. The prophets of Baal prophesied from spirits that were not of God and drew the people away from God. The prophets of Baal are used to cause confusion and doubt of the true and living God.

The prophets of Grove are a different story. The prophets of Grove are of Asherah who is a Canaanite goddess. She was worshipped for fortune and happiness. The worship of Asherah was dancing upon poles and trees near altars. One of the reasons God was so displeased with Ahab is because he made a Grove in Israel. Asherah prophets focus on how happy you will be and they do not encourage holiness, righteousness or obedience unto God, only flesh. They push their listeners into momentary burst of **believing** but give them nothing to actually have faith in. The prophets of Grove are also connected to polytheism called Baalim. These prophets worship and teach multiple gods and beliefs.

The prophets of Baal and the prophets of Grove are an issue today. There are many claiming to be prophets of God that are prophets of a non-existent god. There are many claiming to be prophets of God that are nothing more than idol worshippers using prophetic verbiage. The true prophets of God will have to confront and destroy the false prophetic network that has been built through Baal and Asherah. These false prophets focus on entertaining the flesh of their listeners. It is not about fulfilling the will of God but worship unto a false god through prophesying lies and teaching falsehoods. Baal and Asherah work together to destroy the authenticity of true prophets and prophecy. Their labor is to confuse people with their words of prosperity, without a need to honor God with holy lives.

There will be prophets today and beyond who, like Elijah, will confront and overthrow these false prophets and unholy worship. These prophets will come with a holy sound of destruction to the noise of hell through this false prophetic network and system. The spirit of Elijah is coming upon true prophets of God to be bold and unyielding in the freedom of the people of God. Destroying their altars, images and Groves, will prophets arise to reinstate holy worship to our holy God.

Shemaiah (Not the Overlooked Prophet)
A false prophet showed up during the time of Jeremiah. This false prophet sent a letter to Zephaniah and all who were in Jerusalem, in his own name. This letter lies and says that Zephaniah was chosen to be overseer of the house of the Lord. It goes on to question why he had not rebuked Jeremiah who had been prophesying to him. Shemaiah does not seem pleased with the prophetic word from Jeremiah; that the captivity would be long, build houses and live in them and to plant gardens and eat from them. Zephaniah

read this letter to Jeremiah and God began to speak. God speaks Shemaiah's judgment for speaking falsely. (Jeremiah 29:31-32)

Shemaiah manifests in two ways; falsely prophesying about position and speaking against accurate prophecy. Shemaiah false prophets want to prophesy position to people to interrupt the order of God, to sidetrack the purposes of the kingdom. These false prophets will tell people they are apostles and they are teachers, will tell people they are pastors and they are mayors, the purpose of these false prophecies is to derail destiny. In falsely prophesying about position it causes competition, comparison and disunity. Shemaiah false prophets will always challenge authentic prophecy. The challenge is connected to when the serpent asked Eve, "hath God said?" The purpose is to cause doubt and fear of not hearing God properly. Godly prophecy should never cause doubt.

Barjesus/Elymas
Barjesus is a false prophet and sorcerer. He walked with the deputy of the country, Sergius Paulus. Sergius was an educated and wise man of the faith. He called for Saul (before becoming Paul) and Barnabas because he wanted to hear the word of the Lord. Barjesus opposed Saul and Barnabas because his motive was to draw Sergius from the faith. Saul confronts Barjesus and called him "A child of the devil, an enemy to all righteousness" and asked, "Are you not going to stop perverting the right ways of the Lord?"

Barjesus false prophets are on assignment against faith. Barjesus opposed and withstood Saul and Barnabas because Sergius wanted to hear the word. False prophets will attempt to keep you from the word because the word produces faith. As the assignment is against faith, it will also attack your ability to hear the word that will get you to faith. This false prophet may never speak a word but will oppose you hearing the word of the Lord.

Barjesus is not just a false prophet, but a sorcerer as well. A sorcerer is considered a wise man and a magician. This false prophet, when he does speak will use worldly wisdom to cast spells upon their listeners. They will use anything available to cause their listeners to turn away from God. One of Barjesus' strategies is to get people to deny and turn away from God in the midst of their seeking God.

Ahab and Zedekiah

There are even teams of false prophets. The kingdom of darkness really does attempt to look like the kingdom of God. These particular false prophets are of Babylon. Babylonian prophets speak perverted words as Babylon itself means "Confusion by mixing". These false prophets never speak directly and firmly, but are falsely vague. They attempt to use vocabulary they do not understand and a mix of beliefs. The Babylonian prophets carry spirits that twist communication between heaven and earth and between people. Ahab and Zedekiah work together to pervert communication and prophecy to keep people separated from each other and God. As long as Ahab and Zedekiah are in operation there will be no clarity of what is being said. Ahab and Zedekiah false prophets cause senselessness and disgraceful, immoral and profane actions.

False prophets and false prophecy do not benefit the people of God. As of late, the term false prophet has become taboo. No one wants to judge or discern false prophets, but Jesus told us they were coming. Hell has used a terminology strategy against the ecclesia that caused us to fear speaking against anyone claiming to be a prophet. Anyone claiming to be a prophet that does not line up with the word of God - is not a prophet. Anyone claiming to be a prophet and the words from their mouth or hands never manifest, that is not a prophet. God is not scared of false prophets and neither should His people be. It is time to arise and confront the false, so the true can flourish.

There are many false prophets on television, radio and social media. Over and over again, they speak false words and seduce people from right standing with God. There are too many "prophets of this people" walking the earth. False prophets use the communication system of hell to prey upon their victims. They manipulate and monetize the hurt, ignorance and rebellion of many. False prophets will attempt to obligate their victims to outrageous giving and dedicate service to their ministries but not unto God.

If there arise among you a prophet, or a dreamer of dreams, and giveth thee a sign or a wonder, And the sign or the wonder come to pass, whereof he spake unto thee, saying, Let us go after other gods, which thou hast not known, and let us serve them; Thou shalt not hearken unto the words of that prophet, or that dreamer of dreams: for the Lord your God proveth you, to know whether ye love the Lord your God with all your heart and with all your soul. Ye shall walk after the Lord your God, and fear him, and keep his commandments, and obey his voice, and ye shall serve him, and cleave unto him. And that prophet, or that dreamer of dreams, shall be put to death; because he hath spoken to turn you away from the Lord your God, which brought you out of the land of Egypt, and redeemed you out of the house of bondage, to thrust thee out of the way which the Lord thy God commanded thee to walk in. So shalt thou put the evil away from the midst of thee. (Deuteronomy 13:1-5)

As we have seen, looking at false prophets, they work

against God and those who worship Him. Too often, the church today is too soft on false prophets. All false prophets received a word of death from God because they used His name in vain, prophesied lies and caused His people to err and sin. It is time out for accepting false prophets and rejecting true prophets.

The Conclusion

True prophets, false prophets, popular prophets, overlooked prophets, we have seen them all in *The Biography of Prophets.* The biographies were written to help the church and prophets heal. We have abused each other because we did not understand our assignment with each other. The prophets need the church and vice versa. Neither can fulfill their purpose and destiny if the other is not present.

Some will read this book and wonder, why not talk about Elisha, Jeremiah or Ezekiel. The purpose of this book is to cause hunger for the word of God and His reality of prophets. If you do not see a prophet you want to know about, open the bible and study their lives and ministries to understand them better. We have become so dependent upon the teachers and prophets that our personal study lives are dead. This book is like Elijah stretching out on the dead boy, it was written to resurrect your study life. It is time to take responsibility for your own word intake. If you do not know the authentic word of God, you will not have authentic faith and your hearing with be dull. (Romans 10:17)

Prophet Talk
I want to talk right to the prophets; the emerging, the seasoned, the confused and even the rebelling. God has such a great plan and purpose for your life and ministry. It can be challenging to walk as a prophet but God made you strong on purpose. It is time to put down the flesh and put on Christ, the ultimate prophet. Time to come out of the

caves of bondage, get from under the trees of depression and accept who God says you are.

Something to remember: Prophets have rotating seasons of exposure and obscurity. Obscurity is always a place of deepening, heightening and training the prophet for the next place of revelation and purpose. Exposure is the place of maturity, exercise and manifestation. Learn the season you are in, embrace it and walk it out.

I recently taught a class called, "Strategies Against Prophets". I want to share with you some important strategies of hell against your destiny as a prophet.

1. Sin
Now the works of the flesh are manifest, which are these; Adultery, fornication, uncleanness, lasciviousness, Idolatry, witchcraft, hatred, variance, emulations, wrath, strife, seditions, heresies, Envyings, murders, drunkenness, revellings, and such like: of the which I tell you before, as I have also told you in time past, that they which do such things shall not inherit the kingdom of God. (Galatians 5:19-21)

Sin is missing the mark of obedience, not obeying the directives of God, either written or spoken. Sin, according to Isaiah will hide God's face from us. That is separation. In that separation, HE WILL NOT HEAR us. His ears will be deafened to our communication until we REPENT and RETURN to the righteous way.

We have to guard our relationship and communication with God, not only because we are prophets/prophetic people, but because we are His people. Before you are a prophet, you are His people, His sons (and daughters), your relationship should have good communication skills, both speaking and hearing.

Sin will disconnect your ability to speak to God. Sin will pervert your soul and taint your spirit causing your ability to hear God to be polluted and perverted (usually leading to error).

Hell will paint a false picture of the beauty of sin. The strategy will convince you that everyone sins and will always sin. YOU DO NOT HAVE TO SIN! Sin is a decision that we make willingly to go against the directives/instructions of the Lord. You can live without sin; this is why Jesus died for us. You cannot actually claim to hear God and be actively in sin. Repent and return to the LORD, that communication is not unhindered.

Prophets, you have to learn how to mortify your flesh, crucify your desires and deny yourself to be a vessel of glory. Sin is an agreement against God and His word. Christ went to the cross to free you from sin, not just the judgment of sin. God is requiring prophets to be in intimate relationship with Him and that is not possible where sin is persistent. Sin is a separator from God, as holiness is a separator from sin. As you crucify, mortify and deny your flesh, you are closer to God's requirement of perfection (wholeness, completion, maturity, innocence, healthy) in Him. God does not require perfection outside of Him - but with Him (Deuteronomy 18:13). A sinless life is possible in earth as long as we trust our God to keep us from falling and giving us a way of escape from all temptation (Jude 24; 1 Corinthians 10:13).

2. Jezebel
   One aspect of this strategy is purposed to falsely teach true prophets to make them impure. These teachings cause true prophets to walk in deception and confusion. It teaches

prophetic verbiage but cannot teach the ways of the Lord that would cause prophets to be obedient, faithful and righteous. Teaching is used as a strategy because teaching affects thought, language and even action. As long as the prophets believe lies they cannot access the truth of God, so they cannot speak either.

Another aspect of this strategy is seduction. Seduction before it is sexual, is a drawing away. Jezebel's purpose is to draw prophets away from holiness and righteousness. It wants to entertain the flesh and not engage the spirit. Flesh being entertained is an issue when it causes you to sin. Yes, we are to be balanced; however, a false balance is an abomination unto the Lord. We have to be careful that our seeking of balance does not make us sin. If Jezebel finds an open door to sexual immorality, it will dominate it. From fornication to homosexuality, from masturbation to incest, the strategy is to pervert the prophets; a perverted prophet is not usable by God. Hell knows if prophets are perverted it will prolong the purposes of God but never stop them. *Prophets,* guard your eye-gate, ear-gate and body from all things sexual, that you are not overtaken. You have to remain pure before God and His people to see maximum impact of your ministry.

This strategy seeks to pervert the prophet's worship. Worship is important to God, this why not everyone can worship Him. Worship is reserved for those who are obedient and in covenant with Him, as worship is an expression of covenant. If a prophet's worship is perverted, so is their ability to move in the realm of the Spirit. A prophet who cannot move in the Spirit is like an eagle that cannot soar, unfulfilled.

Jezebel is known as a prophet silencer. However, every prophet can overcome this strategy. The entire strategy works to get the prophet isolated. Isolation is a place, if not ordained by God that becomes a place of hell's victory. Stay in a place of fellowship and sharpening. Stay connected to sources of authentic teaching and impartation. The more teaching you have and the more studying you do with application, the more you will defeat the attempts of Jezebel to silence and pervert you. The word is the greatest weapon against Jezebel. Jehu, the king, defeated Jezebel because of the prophetic word, use the word, swing the sword of the Spirit against Jezebel.

3. Boredom
    Boredom, or being unengaged, is a strategy of hell against the prophets. As long as prophets agree with being bored, they have opened themselves to gluttony and sexual sins and immorality. Boredom will cause prophets to satisfy the feeling of being unengaged or unfilled with eating natural food. It becomes a coping mechanism that leads to gluttony. Gluttony is the sin that we have accepted or only believe that overweight people commit. Gluttony is eating beyond the point of being satisfied. If you are not spiritually satisfied and attempting to satisfy with food, it will never work.

    Boredom rearranged is bedroom. Prophets, hell wants you in the bedroom fornicating, masturbating or engaging with pornography (videos, sexting, phone sex) to keep you in pride, guilt and shame so God cannot use you. Do not allow hell to trap you in a false sense of not having enough to do or not being important. Those are lies whispered to get you to sin against God and your body. Whatever your personal prophetic assignment is, it is important to God and His kingdom and should be important to you.

    Prophets, you have to be open and honest with God, hold nothing back. God can handle your fleshly desires, you cannot. He will always give you a way of escape but you need to be open to His strategy. God will deal with boredom by reigniting passions laid down or igniting what was once unknown. Give God your boredom and let Him let your fire.

4. Questioning God's Voice
    Since Eve in the garden, hell wants the people of God to question everything He has spoken. The first curse released in the earth was "hath God said". This question plagues many believers and prophets today. The strategy is purposed to cause doubt and confusion. If the prophet doubts and is confused by God's voice, they will not speak for Him. If they cannot find the frequency of trust in hearing God, they become silent prophets; ones with an authentic call - never fulfilling it.

    Another aspect of this strategy is manipulating the thinking and analytical nature of prophets and using it against them. When a prophet overthinks or overanalyzes most times they will not obey the instruction given. God is a thinker and an analyzer, so should His prophets be. The prophets must seek God for balance in their thinking and analyzing so they do not end up rebellious and disobedient to God.

    The first step to learning God's voice is learning His word. God will teach you His voice through the verses of Holy Scripture. He will teach you His inflections and you will hear His personal language with you. God is such a communicator. He created a universal language for all and a personal language between you and Him. God is relational and the more you know His word, the more you know His voice.

5. Rejection
    Every prophet has to overcome rejection. Rejection is a

standard attack against prophets. Prophets will have to take their rejection to God, be healed and delivered; because it will happen again. Rejection is constant but prophets must learn to master their response.

Rejection can become the door for the enemy. A prophet that is living in rejection will be susceptible to the flattery of hell and demonic strategies against them and the kingdom of God. Rejection is a bondage that imprisons prophets and restricts them from speaking because it skews their ability to hear God. Many with unresolved rejection issues will find correction as judgment, will be suspicious of true love and question everything with a negative intent. Rejection becomes the root of pessimism and pessimism is a hindrance to true prophetic flow.

Rejection is used to make many people promiscuous. It will create a need for validation and love from all the wrong places. Rejection will cause a strong drive to move in immoral and freaky ways. Rejection will cause an un-verbalized need to satisfy one's self by using other people sexually. Rejection will cause the afflicted to become predators and cause more victims. Rejection is a silent killer because most have no idea how to express that they are rejected. Sex becomes a pacifier to sooth the wounds of rejection. Fornication, adultery, prostitution, pornography and all other forms of sexual immorality are perpetuated through rejected people trying to find themselves through perverted measures. All rejection does not lead to sexual sins but it is one of the more recognizable manifestations. Rejection can also cause depression, isolation, fear and self-inflicted abuse.

To overcome rejection, we all must admit, submit and be delivered. When we admit that we feel rejected, it opens us to the delivering power of God. True admission of rejection is casting that care upon God and releasing it to His hands. After there has been admission, there must be submission. What is there to submit? YOU! You have to submit to God's deliverance and healing process. Every prophet's process is different based upon God's purpose for him or her; do not generalize the deliverance process. After you admit and submit, God will deliver and impart into you. As you are being delivered, God imparts His fearlessness and confidence within you to handle the next rejection situation. God's deliverance will build you to master your responses to all attempts of rejection.

I am reminded of Moses being rejected secretly by Miriam and Aaron. He did not respond in his flesh but in the spirit. They were speaking against him, yet he prayed for Miriam's healing and God healed her. When you have mastered rejection you can pray for those who hurt your flesh but did not wound your spirit.

6. Money
   One of the most intense strategies against prophets is M-O-N-E-Y. Money carries a spirit and if not properly handled, money will destroy a prophet. Money can be used in witchcraft to manipulate and control how the prophet speaks and functions in the earth. Hell presents money to prophets who are challenged financially or financially unwise to compromise their prophetic ability and function for filthy lucre. Those who are challenged or unwise both fall into the category of loving money.

For the love of money is the root of all evil: which while some coveted after, they have erred from the faith, and pierced themselves through with many sorrows.
(1 Timothy 6:10)

Love in this verse means avarice or extreme greed for

wealth or material gain. Prophets who have not learned to rely totally on God will act in avarice when it comes to prophetic ministry, which is evil. Prophets are not to misuse the gift of God for their own gain but are to be compensated for their profession in the kingdom. It is not wrong for prophets to receive offerings, honorariums, etc. however, the spirit in which it is done in, is where they will be judged. The love of money will cause a drawing away from true faith because there is no reliance on the word that produces faith. Drawing away from the faith will produce sorrows that are worse than being challenged financially.

Prophets must learn that God is the best employer ever. He never misses a payment or writes a check that bounces. When God pays you, it is more than you could ever ask for or imagine (Ephesians 3:20). God uses people to compensate prophets so, prophets should not seek man for what only God can supply. Money is not the source of the prophet, God is. Money is only a resource of the source that is from the treasury of heaven. When prophets learn and embrace God as their provider and source, no strategy using money will be accomplished against them.

7. Compromise
   As prophets are God's communicators, they communicate His holiness. Not only do they communicate it, they have to live it. Hell does not want prophets to live holy. They should compromise and mix their stance with worldly views and actions. If prophets are compromised, they will be vessels of erred teachings and prophesying. Prophets cannot compromise His word or His holiness to make the people satisfied or justified in their sin and iniquity.

*Like a muddied fountain and a polluted spring Is a righteous man who yields and **compromises** his integrity before the wicked.* (Proverbs 25:26 AMP)

*He who walks in **integrity** and with moral character walks securely, But he who takes a crooked way will be discovered and punished.* (Proverbs 10:9 AMP)

Prophets have to maintain their integrity in all things. Compromise is seen as perverting the way of the Lord. Prophets must refuse to be convinced that the ways of the Lord are outdated and antiquated and yielding to the way of the world or carnality. Compromise will lead to God's judgment because it is disobedience to His instruction and word.

Most times compromise happens when prophets look to old things as a better way. The only things behind you are those things that were causing you to be an enemy of God. All the things behind you are to be dead and not alive within you, so looking back will resurrect what will destroy you. Do not compromise your future while trying to maintain a dead past.

But Jesus said to him, "No one who puts his hand to the plow and looks back [to the things left behind] is fit for the kingdom of God." (Luke 9:62 AMP)

Compromise is a breach of covenant. *Prophets*, you accepted the terms and conditions of God's will and compromise violates all of them. The only way to repair the breach is to repent and re-submit yourself to His plan and not move from it. *Prophets*, do not commit treason ~ trying to overthrow the Kingdom of God by betraying your allegiance to God and resubmitting to satan and hell.

These are not all the strategies against prophets, but these are standard. Pay attention to how you are attacked, take note and develop a strategy to overcome. No matter what level or dimension you gain access to, hell is going to use the same strategies over and over again.

Father, now in the name of Jesus, I come on behalf of ALL TRUE prophets. Those called of your name to speak forth your will, mind and word in the earth. Strengthen them and make their faces as flint. They need strong backbones to speak your word with authority and power. As you hasten over your word to perform it, You also hasten over your prophets to protect them. Deliver them from rejection, self-inflicted isolation and doubt. Reassure them of their ability to hear, see, write and speak for you. I rebuke the spirit of Ahab, Jezebel and Delilah, the spirits that attempt to kill, usurp and drain the strength and character of your prophets. Strengthen them in their spirit, their faith and reignite passion for intercession. Bring the prophets back to standing between the porch and the altar for your people. And as the prophets are being restored, renewed and upgraded by your presence, sharpen their accuracy and precision in the prophetic and discerning of spirits. We as a people need a true word from you and your prophets have it, cause them to come forth from their caves and SPEAK as only prophets can, in Jesus name, Amen.

There is going to be a deluge of prophets and prophetics in this season. An undeniable manifestation of God's VOICE, GLORY and WILL! As God is cleaning and purifying His vessels, the prophetic will once again carry weight in the earth as it does in Heaven. Prophets, come from out of your caves, get from under those trees and get in place; for the Kingdom of God has need of you.

About the Author

Apostle Javon Rahman Bertrand is anointed and mantled by God for His assignments in the earth realm. He has been redeemed of God and called to the ministry. His testimony is truly a testament to God's strength and his faith. Javon has been delivered and snatched out of a lifestyle of perversion and sin. He is full of wisdom beyond his years and he is a spiritual counselor, a blessing to the Kingdom of God.

By the leading of the Holy Spirit, Javon has birthed *JRB Ministries*, *Embassy Fellowship of Churches*, *Restoration of Love Deliverance Center*, *Watchmen International School of the Prophets* and *The Watchmen Network*. The ministries birthed are mantled to bridge gaps, network other ministries and edify the entire Body of Christ while advancing the Kingdom of God. Javon is apostolically covered and fathered by Apostle/Prophet Alejandro Baldwin and Pure Heart Ministry.

As an author, Javon has released two books to date. *The Watchman* and *The Exposition of the Tabernacle* are best-selling works through his hand and the mouth of God. Javon is also a journalist, having written for Anointed Fire Magazine and currently is a staff writer for *Impact Detroit Magazine*. Javon is also a blogger, his blog is called "Seer's Pen".

He is known as a Man of God that is genuine and says only what thus saith the Lord. He is affectionately known as Apostle J.

Contact Information

You may invite Apostle J to ministry events, speaking engagements, consultations, training sessions or to order signed copies of his books by contacting:

Email: admin@jrbministries.org
Website: www.jrbministries.org
Facebook: Javon Rahman Bertrand
Facebook: JRB Ministries
Twitter: @javonrb
Instagram: @javonrb

All books by Javon Rahman Bertrand are available for purchase on Amazon.com or Barnes & Noble. They are also available as eBooks, please consult the bookstore on your device.

Printed in the USA
CPSIA information can be obtained
at www.ICGtesting.com
CBHW051201070724
11222CB00024BA/861